── THE ──
VEGAN MEAT
COOKBOOK

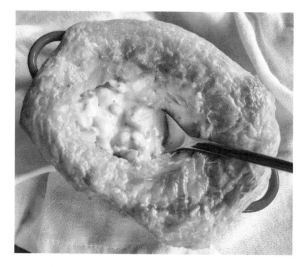

— THE —
VEGAN MEAT
COOKBOOK

100 Impossibly Delicious, Alternative-Meat Recipes

— ISABEL MINUNNI —

STERLING EPICURE
New York

STERLING EPICURE
New York

An Imprint of Sterling Publishing Co., Inc.
122 Fifth Avenue
New York, NY 10011

ISBN 978-1-4549-4174-3
978-1-4549-4175-0 (e-book)

Distributed in Canada by Sterling Publishing Co., Inc.
c/o Canadian Manda Group, 664 Annette Street
Toronto, Ontario M6S 2C8, Canada
Distributed in the United Kingdom by GMC Distribution Services
Castle Place, 166 High Street, Lewes, East Sussex BN7 1XU, England
Distributed in Australia by NewSouth Books
University of New South Wales, Sydney, NSW 2052, Australia

For information about custom editions, special sales,
and premium and corporate purchases, please contact
Sterling Special Sales at 800-805-5489
or specialsales@sterlingpublishing.com.

Manufactured in Malaysia

2 4 6 8 10 9 7 5 3 1

sterlingpublishing.com

Cover design by Elizabeth Mihaltse
Photo credits are on page 164

CONTENTS

INTRODUCTION:
THE RIGHT TIME FOR PLANT-BASED MEATS

What is "Plant-Based Meat" Anyway?

Alternative proteins are everywhere: but what exactly does the paradoxical term "plant-based meat" or "vegan meat" mean? Before getting started with how to cook using these wonder products, allow us to answer your burning questions.

Why is Everything Vegan All of a Sudden?

In October 2019, the Awesome Burger hit griddles and grills all over the country. When it hit the hot metal, the patty sizzled and smoked like a proper burger, and once the outside was pleasantly browned, the inside was still juicy and pink. Earlier that year, Burger King customers were filmed for a commercial praising the taste of a Whopper and proclaiming that only real meat could do for the taste buds what this burger was doing. But in all of these instances, the burger was made entirely from plant proteins.

Thanks to growing concerns among the global population that our appetite for meat has created a cycle of environmental harm, those who might not have turned to vegetarianism or veganism for health or animal welfare concerns are cutting down on their meat intake. According to a survey from the Sentience Institute, 54 percent of people in the U.S. are attempting to curb their carnivorism, placing plant-based meats like the Awesome and Impossible™ Burgers in heavy demand. Plant-based chicken, pork, ground beef, and more are all available or on the horizon and promise to take some of the strain off the global meat industry.

Did This Come Out of Nowhere?

Not really. Vegetarian meat alternatives are nothing new: the health conscious and those with ethical concerns about meat have been chowing down on dishes like the Boca Burger and the veggie patty for decades, and there are tofu-based alternatives for just about every dish imaginable (here's looking at you, Tofurky®). In fact, John Harvey Kellogg, the man who popularized breakfast cereal in the U.S., created a "meatless meat," Nuttose, that he sold to sanatoriums in the late 1800s. Since its discovery in 1967, a high-protein fungus called *Fusarium venenatum* has been used as a meat alternative. In the 1980s, the Gardenburger was created with leftover vegetables and rice pilaf and in 1998 their sales skyrocketed after a commercial aired during the *Seinfeld* finale. Around the same time, the vegan loaf company Field Roast began their plant-based meat operations, which include popular chicken and sausage alternatives, as well as plant-based cheeses.

The plant-based meat industry took its present form, however, in 2011 with the founding of Redwood City, California's Impossible Foods. The goal of this force in alternative protein was new for the vegetarian food industry: They didn't just want to make a vegan meat product; they wanted to make a vegan meat product that mimicked both the taste and nutritional benefits of real meat. Five years later, their signature product, the Impossible Burger, was introduced.

In 2019, the company announced its next goal to create a whole-cut Impossible Steak, which would, along with new arrival Impossible Pork, further disrupt the meat industry.

OK, It's Not Meat. So What Is It Exactly?

While each plant-based meat alternative has its own recipe, there is one element, whose role was discovered by Impossible Foods, that will probably be found in all plant-based "meats" moving forward: Heme. This molecule gives blood its color and in mammals helps carry oxygen throughout the body. It's also what makes meat behave the way it does. By harnessing the molecule, plant matter can be tricked into acting like meat when it's cooked. By extracting heme from the leghemoglobin molecules found in parts of soy plants, Impossible Foods was able to source heme without using animal products. The iron-rich molecule even helps mimic the taste of real meat. A base of heme-containing soy is then added to yeast for a fermentation that recalls the early beer making process. Textured soy or wheat gives the burger its heft, and coconut fat flecks offer the distinctive marbling found in real meat. In 2016 the burger began appearing at upscale restaurants in New York, Los Angeles, and San Francisco. Before long, chains like Bareburger had picked up the burger and it was a nationwide sensation. Mega-chains like Burger King and Dunkin' were soon offering Impossible Burgers and sausage patties. The FDA soon sided with a panel of experts that had declared the Impossible Burger safe. Kosher and Halal certification followed close behind. The non-meat meat era had begun in earnest: no longer were the health conscious and ethically minded forced to choke down bland patties of leftover veggies and rice.

And That Means It's Healthier?

Mostly. Its sudden popularity has given plant-based meat products quite a reputation in the food world, but it's not a silver bullet for your health and the environment all at once. Plant-based meat alternatives are a great innovation in culinary science and one that could change the way the world consumes. And while there are a number of health benefits compared to real meat, the biggest impact plant-based alternatives have had on the industry has been on its environmental footprint. Impossible Foods, for example, claims that creating their burger uses 95 percent less land and 74 percent less water than creating one from a cow, while emitting 87 percent fewer greenhouse gases. For many observers, the animal farming industry is tagged as one of the biggest culprits in our worsening climate crisis, making a meat alternative that actually tastes like the real thing one of our strongest weapons in that fight.

So plant-based meat alternatives could very well help save the world if enough people start eating them regularly. But some caution is required before you begin treating them like they're also as miraculous for your body. Impossible Burgers, for example, contain less cholesterol and total fat, as well as fewer calories, than their cow-based cousins. But they do contain more sodium than an unseasoned beef patty, as well as more saturated fat. Basically, whether or not plant-based meat is significantly better for you than real meat depends on the individual. For those whose blood pressure is on target but with slightly high cholesterol, it's a great idea. For someone with the opposite problems, real or plant-based is pretty much a toss-up. In short, plant-based meat is better for us in that it can help solve some of the problems that threaten humanity. But anyone telling you it's a magic potion for all of your maladies is probably selling you something. Like most everything else, plant-based meat alternatives should be enjoyed in moderation as part of a balanced plate.

The Benefits of a Plant-Based Approach

It's not just you: Lots of people are taking a second look at going vegan. Here's what they stand to gain.

Veganism Isn't New, So Why is It Important All of a Sudden?

The recent rise in veganism has two main causes: health and ethics. People have never been short of ideas for trimming waistlines, and with its emphasis on natural and plant-based foods, veganism is an easy sell. But more important in recent years than personal health has been environmental health, and more people are going vegan today as part of an effort to curb the impact of the meat industry. According to *The Guardian*, in 2016 we bought 317 million metric tons of meat, with the greenhouse gas emissions from that process accounting for an estimated 18 percent of the global total. A 2010 global study of water use in agriculture found that while fruits and vegetables averaged a water consumption of 962 liters per kg and 322 l/kg, respectively, beef required 15,415 l/kg. Livestock is also the world's largest user of land resources. As questions about the overuse of resources, overcrowding of cities, and the worsening of climate change continue, a reckoning with the sheer size of our meat appetite isn't a longshot. Those going vegan for environmental reasons are simply trying to get ahead of the game.

How to Shop Like a Vegan

Whether you're doing a short-term vegan experiment or looking to switch to a cruelty-free diet full-time, it's important to create a shopping list that covers all of your nutritional bases without any of the animal products you're used to eating. Your vegan shopping list should include plenty of the following: fresh vegetables (which will make up the bulk of your new diet), fresh fruit, frozen and canned fruits and vegetables for convenience, plenty of soy products like tofu and edamame for protein, dairy alternatives like dairy-free yogurts and nut milks, and whole grains. It's also important to make up for the vitamin B12 you'll be losing, either by eating fortified foods or taking a B12 supplement. Don't worry, as you'll see in our recipe section beginning on page 9, part of veganism going mainstream is that delicious plant-based products are available to re-create all of your non-vegan favorites.

Plant-Based Meat: The Science Behind the Products

Some of the most talked about recent additions to the vegan world are products like the Impossible Burger that emulate the taste and texture of meat without any animals being harmed in the process. By offering a vegan alternative to the country's most beloved foodstuff, the burger has made veganism a more realistic choice for millions. By making the diet more accessible and less penitential, products like Impossible's are paving the way for a revolution in the way humans consume. While no healthy diet consists of hamburgers or sausage every day, being able to re-create our favorite comfort foods convincingly without meat gives us more options to avoid meat when we do crave a Whopper or a sausage gumbo. And in addition to the vast environmental benefits of eschewing meat for plants, you can also expect to see less cholesterol in your alternative proteins. Some plant-based meat products do contain a fair amount of sodium in their seasoning, so those who are sensitive to salt should always check the label before buying.

Where You'll Feel It Most

According to a January 2020 BBC interview with Marco Springmann, senior researcher of environmental sustainability and public health at the University of Oxford, veganism has stood the test of time despite its detractors because it really does work. "We've found that the vegan diet could be one of the healthiest diets, outperforming pescatarian and vegetarian, because the vegan diet is higher in fruit, vegetables, and legumes and the health benefits from this compensate for anything else," he said. By basing a diet around natural foods like whole grains and vegetables of all colors (meaning you're getting a wide range of vitamins and other nutrients), vegans typically consume less of those harmful processed foods and extra fats. The availability of plant-based meat products allows those who are hungry for the meat products they've worked so hard to cut out to maintain their new lifestyle with minimal impact.

Maximize Your (Alternative) Meat

The fact is, exactly how much plant-based alternatives mimic real meat is up to you and your skills in the kitchen. But don't worry: these tips will put you on the right track.

Stay Alert

Plant-based meat alternatives tend to brown a bit more quickly than real meat, so make sure you don't let them overcook. A big part of ensuring products such as Impossible Meat mimic the real thing is maintaining a nice pink color and making sure all of the juices don't cook off.

Get Creative

Test out different cooking methods. You can panfry, grill, griddle, or even bake your Impossible Burger, for example, as long as the internal temperature reaches 165°F.

Spice Up Your Salads

A great way to make alternative beef a part of a healthier meal is to crumble some over your favorite salad greens or whole grain bowls, but for the best results you should thoroughly brown your protein beforehand.

Don't Panic If You're in a Rush

Impossible Foods does recommend that you thaw their products before cooking, but you can cook alternative protein from frozen by simply adding some time on each side. So if you're strapped for time, don't worry about thawing it out—just cook it.

Don't Smash That Burger

Smashburgers, which are pressed flat against a griddle to achieve a crispy outer layer and perfectly cooked inner layer, are extremely popular with carnivores at the moment. But even though the temptation to replicate them with alternative protein might be strong, doing so will force all the juices and fatty bits that make your burger seem real to melt away onto the griddle.

Go for the Glutamates

When people talk about vegan food mimicking classic flavors from less ethical dishes, a lot of the credit goes to the savory flavor known as umami. According to food scientist J. Kenji Lopez-Alt, writing in *The New York Times*, "It's no coincidence that the most successful dishes I've made with plant-based meat have included ingredients like mushrooms, soy sauce, tomatoes, and aged cheeses. All of these ingredients are rich in glutamates, the chemical compounds largely responsible for the mouthwatering savory flavor."

Think Eastern

Lopez-Alt also points out that one of the best applications for plant-based beef alternatives is in Chinese dishes that use meat sparingly to add flavor and texture to the overall dish. "Sichuan classics like dan dan noodles and mapo tofu, for instance, can be made completely vegan without any noticeable loss of flavor or texture," he writes.

BREAKFAST

Thanksgiving-Style Breakfast Bake

All the flavors you love in the perfect morning casserole.

Serves 4–6

2 tablespoons (30ml) olive oil

1.5 ounces (42g) vegan seasoned stuffing mix (or about ¼ cup seasoned bread cubes)

1 onion, diced

1 stalk celery, diced

½ red pepper, diced

½ teaspoon dried sage

¼ teaspoon dried thyme

2 Beyond® Meat Beyond Sausage links

1 cup (113g) grated vegan cheddar cheese

10 servings vegan egg substitute, uncooked (like JUST)

Preheat the oven to 350°F (180°C).

Brush a large baking dish with oil. Place the stuffing mix into the baking dish.

In a medium skillet over medium heat, add the remaining oil and cook the onions, celery, red pepper, sage, and thyme. Cook until the vegetables are tender.

Cook the sausage according to the package directions. Cut into bite-size pieces.

Place the cooked vegetables, sausage, cheese, and egg into the baking dish and mix with the stuffing mix. Place in the preheated oven and cook for about 30 minutes or until the eggs are set.

CALORIES: 206.8; **TOTAL FAT:** 8.9g; **SODIUM:** 549.6mg; **TOTAL CARBOHYDRATES:** 17.5g; **DIETARY FIBER:** 5.9g; **SUGARS:** 2.2g; **PROTEIN:** 7.8g

Polenta Shakshuka Breakfast Bowl

A modern twist on the comfort-fueled Middle Eastern dish, the polenta adds a texture that will have you coming back for thirds.

Serves 4

5 cups (1.25 liters) almond milk

1 cup (128g) quick yellow cornmeal

2 8.5-ounce (241g) Gardein™ Shakshuka Breakfast Bowls

¼ cup (28g) grated vegan Parmesan cheese

4–5 fresh basil leaves, chopped

In a medium-size saucepan over medium-high heat, bring the milk and cornmeal to a simmer and let cook until tender, stirring often, around 5–8 minutes.

Cook the breakfast bowls according to the package directions.

Place an equal amount of the polenta into 4 serving bowls, top each with an equal amount of the cooked breakfast bowls. Garnish each bowl with the Parmesan cheese and basil.

CALORIES: 357.4; TOTAL FAT: 11.2g; SODIUM: 642.1mg; TOTAL CARBOHYDRATES: 54.9g; DIETARY FIBER: 6.7g; SUGARS: 11.4g; PROTEIN: 17.1g

Italian-Style Breakfast Crepes Bake

Flaky crepes are the perfect vessel for these unbeatable flavors of the Mediterranean.

Serves 4–5

¾ cup (96g) all-purpose flour

¼ cup (32g) whole wheat flour

⅛ teaspoon salt

1½ cups (350ml) unsweetened almond milk

¼ cup (60ml) unsweetened applesauce

2 tablespoons (30ml) olive oil, plus extra for the pan

10 Field Roast® Wild Mushroom Deli Slices

10 Field Roast Tomato Cayenne Chao Slices

5 servings vegan scrambled eggs (your favorite brand or homemade)

½ cup (120ml) vegan tomato sauce

½ cup (56g) vegan mozzarella cheese, shredded

1 small bunch fresh basil, chopped

In a blender, blend the flours, salt, milk, applesauce, and oil until smooth.

Preheat the oven to 350°F (180° C).

In a nonstick skillet over medium-low heat, pour ¼ cup (60ml) of batter and swirl it around in the pan. Cook the crepe for 1 minute, flip with a spatula, and cook for another minute. Remove from the pan and continue making the remaining crepes.

Fill each crepe with a slice of the Wild Mushroom and the Tomato Cayenne Chao and the prepared eggs. Roll up the crepe and place in an oven-safe dish, top with the sauce and cheese, place in the preheated oven, and cook until the crepes are hot and the cheese has melted (about 10–15 minutes). Garnish with basil.

CALORIES: 246.1; TOTAL FAT: 9.6g; SODIUM: 632.4mg; TOTAL CARBOHYDRATES: 26.7g; DIETARY FIBER: 7.6g; SUGARS: 4.6g; PROTEIN: 10.3g

Bacon Jam Breakfast Panini

A vegan-friendly bacon jam made from scratch
is just the beginning of this hearty meal.

Serves 4

Seitan Bacon Jam

8 slices Seitan Bacon (your favorite brand)

1 large onion, diced

2 cloves garlic, minced

⅓ cup (80ml) apple cider vinegar

½ cup (100g) coconut sugar

¼ cup (60ml) pure maple syrup

½ cup (120ml) brewed coffee

Panini

8 slices vegan Italian-style panini bread

2 cups (226g) grated vegan cheddar cheese

1 cup (28g) fresh spinach

1 cup (180g) sliced cherry tomatoes

4 servings vegan scrambled eggs (your favorite brand or homemade)

Olive oil

In a large nonstick frying pan, cook the bacon according to the package directions. Remove from the pan and set aside.

In the same pan, add oil and cook the onions and garlic on medium heat until softened. Add the remaining bacon jam ingredients and simmer, stirring often, until the mixture has reduced and become thick. Stir in the cooked bacon.

Transfer the mixture to a food processor and pulse the ingredients together until you reach a coarsely chopped consistency.

Top 4 slices of bread with half of the cheese. Top each with the spinach, tomatoes, eggs, bacon jam, and the remaining cheese. Top each with the remaining bread. Brush the bread with olive oil on both sides and cook according to the panini-maker manufacturer's directions.

CALORIES: 420.9; **TOTAL FAT:** 10.6g; **SODIUM:** 838.7mg; **TOTAL CARBOHYDRATES:** 58.1g; **DIETARY FIBER:** 2.9g; **SUGARS:** 23.6g; **PROTEIN:** 23.9g

Breakfast Burger

The drive-thru taste you love in a fresh-out-of-bed package.

Serves 4

4 Impossible Burgers

5 tablespoons (75ml) vegan ketchup

2 tablespoons (30ml) Sriracha

4 vegan bagels or croissants

4 servings prepared vegan eggs (your favorite brand or homemade)

4 slices vegan cheddar cheese

8 slices vegan bacon, cooked

12–16 vegan Tater Tots, cooked

Cook the burgers according to the package directions.

In a small bowl, mix together the ketchup and Sriracha.

Toast the bottom half of the 4 bagels or croissants, top each with a cooked burger, an equal amount of the eggs, cheese, bacon, Tater Tots, and Sriracha ketchup. Top each with the top half of the bagel or croissant.

CALORIES: 623.2; TOTAL FAT: 33.9g; SODIUM: 1,477mg; TOTAL CARBOHYDRATES: 47.8g; DIETARY FIBER: 17.8g; SUGARS: 2.8g; PROTEIN: 30.7g

Breakfast Hand Pies

When you need a big meal you can take to go, you can't
go wrong with these handheld pockets of flavor.

Serves 4–6

4 servings scrambled vegan eggs
(your favorite or homemade)

10 ounces (283g) cooked vegan ham

2 sheets puff pastry

2 tablespoons (30ml) olive oil

1 cup (240ml) vegan cheese sauce

Preheat the oven to 400°F (200°C).

Cook the eggs and ham according to the
package directions and set aside.

Cut the puff pastry sheets into 12 equal
pieces. Brush a parchment-lined baking sheet
with some olive oil and place 6 pieces of the
dough onto the sheet.

Top each piece of dough with the cooked
eggs, ham, and cheese, leaving the edges
free. Place a piece of dough on top of the
filling and pinch the edges with a fork to close
the pies. Brush the top of each pie with the
remaining olive oil.

Place the pies into the preheated oven and
cook for about 15–20 minutes or until the
pastry is lightly browned.

CALORIES: 248.7; TOTAL FAT: 14.8g; SODIUM: 447.8mg; TOTAL
CARBOHYDRATES: 14.6g; DIETARY FIBER: 6.3g; SUGARS: 1.1g;
PROTEIN: 12.4g

HOMEMADE VEGAN SCRAMBLED EGGS

Frying up crumbled extra-firm tofu with
nutritional yeast and seasoning makes
a delicious and simple dish of vegan
scrambled eggs; you can even mix in
turmeric for color.

Breakfast Tacos

Perfect for Tuesdays or any other time, these tasty tacos have south-of-the-border flavor with a California twist.

Serves 4

12 ounces (340g) firm tofu

1 teaspoon beet powder

3 teaspoons (15ml) vegan ham-flavored broth base

1 tablespoon (15ml) olive oil

4 vegan taco shells

4 servings vegan scrambled eggs (your favorite brand or homemade)

1 cup (113g) vegan cheddar cheese, shredded

½ cup (90g) small tomatoes, diced

½ cup (120ml) vegan hollandaise sauce (your favorite brand or homemade)

Preheat the oven to 350°F (175°C).

Wrap the tofu in a cheesecloth or a clean kitchen towel and squeeze as much liquid as you can from the tofu. In a medium-size bowl, break the tofu up into crumbles and mix in the beet powder and broth base, coating the tofu evenly and thoroughly. Brush a parchment-lined baking sheet with some olive oil, and place the tofu mixture onto the baking sheet.

Bake the tofu in the preheated oven for 15 minutes, turn the baking sheet 180 degrees, and continue to cook for another 15 minutes. Stir the tofu and cook another 10 minutes or until set and no longer wet.

Fill each taco shell evenly with the tofu, prepared eggs, cheese, and tomatoes. Top each with an equal amount of the hollandaise sauce.

CALORIES: 318.7; TOTAL FAT: 17.9g; SODIUM: 600.4mg; TOTAL CARBOHYDRATES: 24.8g; DIETARY FIBER: 9.2g; SUGARS: 1.1g; PROTEIN: 14.5g

Sausage Pancake with Apple Pie Syrup

Enjoy the tastes of fall in a dish that's great all year round.

Serves 4

4 links Field Roast Apple Maple Breakfast Sausage

vegan pancake mix

¾ cup (180ml) pure maple syrup

1 apple, diced

½ teaspoon cinnamon

½ teaspoon vanilla

⅛ teaspoon nutmeg

1 tablespoon canola oil

Cook the sausage according to the package directions. Cut in half lengthwise.

Make the pancake batter according to the package directions for 8 large pancakes.

In a small saucepan, add the syrup, apples, cinnamon, vanilla, and nutmeg on medium-low heat. Cook until the apples are tender, stirring often.

Put the oil into a nonstick skillet on medium heat, place a sausage-shaped pancake onto the skillet, top each pancake with a sausage half, and cover with more batter. Cook until lightly browned, flip, and cook the other side until lightly brown and cooked through.

Top each sausage pancake with the apple pie syrup.

CALORIES: 388.0; **TOTAL FAT:** 12.1g; **SODIUM:** 523.7mg; **TOTAL CARBOHYDRATES:** 55.4g; **DIETARY FIBER:** 4g; **SUGARS:** 33.9g; **PROTEIN:** 17.1g

Szechuan Steak and Tofu Scrambled Eggs

Spicy and filling, this stovetop scramble will stick with you till dinner.

Serves 4

10 ounces (283g) Gardein Szechuan Beefless Strips

2 16-ounce (454g) packages firm tofu

1 tablespoon (15ml) olive oil

4 tablespoons (45g) nutritional yeast

½ teaspoon ground turmeric

½ teaspoon pepper

½ teaspoon pink Himalayan salt

½ teaspoon onion powder

3 tablespoons (9g) fresh chives, chopped

3 tablespoons (45ml) non-dairy milk, unsweetened and unflavored

Cook the beefless strips according to the package directions.

Wrap the tofu in a cheesecloth or clean kitchen towel and squeeze the liquid from the tofu as much as possible.

In a large skillet over medium heat, heat the oil until the skillet is hot but not smoking. Crumble the tofu into the hot skillet. Cook, stirring frequently, for 3–4 minutes or until the water from the tofu is mostly gone.

Add the nutritional yeast, turmeric, pepper, salt, onion powder, and chives. Cook for about 5 minutes, stirring constantly.

Pour the nondairy milk into the skillet and stir to mix. Serve immediately with the Szechuan strips.

CALORIES: 340.4; TOTAL FAT: 17g; SODIUM: 240.8mg; TOTAL CARBOHYDRATES: 20.4g; DIETARY FIBER: 5.1g; SUGARS: 1.7g; PROTEIN: 31.4g

Smoked Tomato Avocado Toast

Perfectly portioned for an AM kick-starter,
this dish is best when made fresh.

Serves 4

2 avocados

1 tablespoon (15ml) lemon juice

4 slices vegan bread, toasted

4 Field Roast Smoked Tomato Deli Slices

4 servings prepared vegan scrambled eggs (your favorite brand or homemade)

½ cup (28 g) roasted chickpeas

¼ cup (37g) red onion, sliced

½ cup (16g) alfalfa sprouts

¼ cup (60ml) vegan hollandaise sauce

hot sauce (optional)

In a small bowl, combine the avocados and lemon juice and mash with a fork.

Place an even amount of the mashed avocado on top of each piece of toast. Top the avocado with a slice of Smoked Tomato Deli, an equal amount of the eggs, chickpeas, onions, and sprouts. Drizzle each with hollandaise sauce and hot sauce if desired.

CALORIES: 359.7; TOTAL FAT: 20.6g; SODIUM: 446.8mg; TOTAL CARBOHYDRATES: 32.2g; DIETARY FIBER: 11.7g; SUGARS: 6.4g; PROTEIN: 15.1g

Southwest Stuffed French Toast

Equal parts savory and sweet, this dish gets
an extra kick when you add fresh jalapeño.

Serves 4

....

4 slices vegan Texas toast or
vegan bread, cut thick

12 ounces (340g) Gardien
Southwest Saus'age &
Veggie Breakfast Bowl

¾ cup (84g) vegan cheddar
cheese, shredded

3 servings vegan eggs,
uncooked

1 tablespoon (15ml) olive oil

½ cup (120ml) pure maple
syrup

1 jalapeño, diced with seeds
removed (optional)

Cut a pocket into each slice of the bread.

Cook the breakfast bowls according to the package
directions. Stuff each pocket equally with the sausage
mixture.

Place the stuffed bread into the eggs and let soak into
the bread. Place in a hot pan with oil and cook until
lightly brown on both sides.

In a small bowl, mix the syrup and jalapeño together
and serve with the French toast.

CALORIES: 384.9; TOTAL FAT: 15.8g; SODIUM: 809.5mg; TOTAL
CARBOHYDRATES: 44.3g; DIETARY FIBER: 7g; SUGARS: 21.7g; PROTEIN: 15.3g

Chipped Beef and Eggs Breakfast

Your morning just got a little brighter with this easy-to-prepare crowd-pleaser.

Serves 4

2 cups (475ml) vegan beef broth

¼ teaspoon dried thyme

¼ teaspoon dried parsley

2 tablespoons (14g) cornstarch

3 tablespoons (45ml) water

10 ounces (283g) Beyond Meat Beyond Beef Crumbles, Beefy

4 large vegan biscuits (your favorite brand or homemade)

4 servings vegan eggs (your favorite brand or homemade—see Tip below)

2 tablespoons (6g) fresh chives or green onions, chopped

1 tablespoon red bell peppers, chopped

In a saucepan over medium-high heat, bring the broth to a simmer. Add in the thyme and parsley.

In a small bowl, mix together the cornstarch and water, then add it into the simmering broth to thicken.

Cook the beef crumbles according to the package directions. Add to the sauce.

Place an even amount of the chipped beef over the biscuits, top with an equal amount of the eggs. Garnish with the chives and peppers.

CALORIES: 203.9; TOTAL FAT: 6.5g; SODIUM: 672.7mg; TOTAL CARBOHYDRATES: 23.3g; DIETARY FIBER: 4.3g; SUGARS: 1.5g; PROTEIN: 13.5g

HOMEMADE EGG SUBSTITUTE

Mix 1 tablespoon of chia or flax seed with 2½ tablespoons of water for a quick egg substitute. Mashed bananas, applesauce, and silken tofu are all good egg substitutes for baking.

Spicy Morning Breakfast Bowl

Peperoncini add a bit of heat to this collection of winning flavors.

Serves 4

4 cups (1 liter) potatoes, chopped

½ red pepper, diced

1 small onion, diced

4 peperoncini peppers, sliced (extra for garnish, if desired)

2 tablespoons (30ml) olive oil

½ teaspoon salt

½ teaspoon pepper

4 links Beyond Meat Beyond Sausage, Hot Italian

2 cups (226g) grated vegan cheese

4 servings vegan scrambled eggs (your favorite brand or homemade)

1 cup (240ml) vegan tomato sauce

Preheat the oven to 350°F (180°C).

Place the potatoes, peppers, onions, and peperoncini onto a parchment-lined sheet pan. Drizzle with the oil and season with salt and pepper. Place in the preheated oven and cook until the potatoes are tender (about 15-20 minutes).

Cook the sausage according to the package directions. Cut the cooked sausages in half, then into ½-inch (12mm) pieces.

Place an equal amount of the cooked potatoes into 4 bowls, top each with an equal amount of the sausage, cheese, eggs, and sauce. Garnish each bowl with peperoncini, if desired.

CALORIES: 421.7; **TOTAL FAT:** 20.2g; **SODIUM:** 827.4mg; **TOTAL CARBOHYDRATES:** 38.3g; **DIETARY FIBER:** 12.0g; **SUGARS:** 3.5g; **PROTEIN:** 20.4g

Bloody Mary Breakfast

Feel free to pair these waffles with the boozy brunch cocktail they're named after.

Serves 4

Vegan waffle mix

2 links Field Roast
  Mexican Chipotle
  Sausage

4 slices vegan bacon

4 slices vegan cheese

4 romaine lettuce leaves,
  cut to fit mini waffles

3 tablespoons (45ml)
  ketchup

12 cherry tomatoes

4 jalapeño peppers

1 slice lime

celery salt, for the rim

4 stalks celery

32 ounces (1 liter) vegan
  Bloody Mary mix

Make enough waffle batter to make 24 mini waffles according to the package directions, and make the waffles.

Cook the sausage according to the package directions. Cut it into ½-inch (12mm) rounds.

Cook the bacon according to the package directions. Cut the bacon slices into 3 equal pieces.

Place a cooked sausage round onto a mini waffle. Top with cheese, lettuce, bacon, and ketchup, then top with another mini waffle. With a large skewer, pierce the mini sandwich, and then top with a cherry tomato. Continue until you have 3 sandwiches on the skewer. Prepare 3 more skewers. Top each skewer with a jalapeño pepper.

Rub the rims of 4 glasses with lime and dip each into celery salt. Fill the glasses with the Bloody Mary mix, and place a skewer and celery stalk in each glass.

CALORIES: 321.1; **TOTAL FAT:** 13.0g; **SODIUM:** 900.0mg; **TOTAL CARBOHYDRATES:** 35.3g; **DIETARY FIBER:** 4.6g; **SUGARS:** 11.7g; **PROTEIN:** 15.6g

*Can be served with vodka or tequila.

Breakfast Bagel Nachos

A great way to start your day (or end your evening!),
these nachos are addictive and guilt-free.

Serves 4

12 ounces (340g) Impossible Pork

7 ounces (198g) vegan bagel chips

4 servings vegan scrambled eggs (your favorite brand or homemade, see page 16)

1 cup (113g) vegan cheddar cheese, shredded

½ cup (75g) onion, diced

½ cup (100g) tomatoes, diced

¼ cup (32g) black olives, sliced

¼ cup (24g) jalapeños, sliced

2 tablespoons (6g) chives, chopped

½ cup (120ml) vegan sour cream

½ cup (240g) guacamole

Preheat the oven to 350°F (180°C).

Break the pork into small pieces and cook according to the package directions.

Place the bagel chips on an oven-safe platter. Top the chips with the cooked pork, prepared eggs, cheese, onions, tomatoes, olives, and jalapeños. Place in the oven until the cheese melts. Take out of the oven, and top with chives, sour cream, and guacamole.

CALORIES: 499.8; TOTAL FAT: 26.8g; SODIUM: 1980mg; TOTAL CARBOHYDRATES: 42.2g; DIETARY FIBER: 12.3g; SUGARS: 2.4g; PROTEIN: 21.6g

Sausage Stuffed Breakfast Bread

The great thing about a dish like this one is the leftovers
are amazing—assuming you have any.

Serves 4

8 ounces (226g) Impossible Pork

1 vegan pizza dough

4 servings vegan eggs (your
favorite brand or homemade)

1½ cups (170g) vegan mozzarella
cheese, shredded

2 cups (650g) cooked potatoes,
diced

1 tablespoon (15ml) olive oil, plus
1 teaspoon (5 ml) for brushing

In a small pan, break the pork into small pieces
and cook according to the package directions.

Preheat the oven to 350°F (180°C).

Lay the dough out in a 13x10-inch (33 x 23cm)
triangle. Place the cooked sausage, eggs, cheese,
and potatoes evenly onto the dough leaving a
1-inch (2.5cm) border free of ingredients. Grease a
parchment-lined sheet pan with olive oil. Roll the
dough around filling, jelly-roll style, and place on
the greased sheet pan, seam side down. Brush the
top of the bread with the remaining olive oil.

Place in the preheated oven and cook for about
20 minutes or until the bread is lightly browned
and crispy.

CALORIES: 636.8; TOTAL FAT: 37.2g; SODIUM: 890mg; TOTAL
CARBOHYDRATES: 55.8g; DIETARY FIBER: 15.6g; SUGARS: 1.6g;
PROTEIN: 23.9g

Sausage and Pineapple Waffles

With two great tastes that blend incredibly well, this is another savory-sweet stunner you'll quickly add to your regular rotation.

Serves 4–5

3 tablespoons (21g) arrowroot

1½ cups (350ml) almond milk, unsweetened

1 tablespoon (15ml) apple cider vinegar

1½ cups (192g) all-purpose flour

1 tablespoon (7g) baking powder

½ teaspoon salt

3 tablespoons (37g) coconut sugar

¼ cup (60ml) olive oil

1 teaspoon vanilla extract

8 ounces (226g) Impossible Pork

¾ cup (123g) pineapple, diced

½ cup (118ml) pure maple syrup

In a large bowl, combine the arrowroot, milk, vinegar, flour, baking powder, salt, coconut sugar, oil, and vanilla. Set aside.

Break the pork into small pieces and cook according to the package directions

Place the sausage and pineapple into the waffle mixture.

Preheat a waffle iron. Cook the waffles according to the manufacturer's directions. Serve with syrup.

CALORIES: 283.9; TOTAL FAT: 4.8g; SODIUM: 305.8mg; TOTAL CARBOHYDRATES: 55.1g; DIETARY FIBER: 2.5g; SUGARS: 22.1g; PROTEIN: 6.9g

Cheeseburger Omelet

Egg and cheese lovers will flip over this beefy breakfast dish.

Serves 4

....

1 tablespoon (15ml) olive oil

1 small onion, diced

10 ounces (283g) Beyond Meat Beyond Beef Crumbles, Beefy

¼ cup (60ml) vegan relish

1 small tomato, diced

4 servings vegan eggs (your favorite brand or homemade, see page TK)

4 Field Roast Creamy Original Chao Slices

In a small pan on medium-low heat, add the oil and cook the onions until tender.

Add the beef crumbles and cook according to the package directions.

In a medium bowl, mix together the cooked onions, cooked beef, relish, and tomatoes.

Make the eggs according to the package directions for omelets. Stuff the omelets with an equal amount of beef mixture and top with a slice of the Chao.

CALORIES: 258.5; TOTAL FAT: 15.8g; SODIUM: 571.5mg; TOTAL CARBOHYDRATES: 14.8g; DIETARY FIBER: 7.5g; SUGARS: 1.9g; PROTEIN: 11.8g

Sausage Bites

Make a double batch of these tasty morsels—
you're going to need them!

Serves 4

2 tablespoons (30ml) olive oil

2 onions, sliced

9 ounces (255g) Gardein Sliced
Italian Saus'age

¼ cup (60g) spicy brown mustard

¼ cup (81g) vegan blackberry jam

In a nonstick skillet over low heat, add oil and
cook the onions, stirring often, until brown
and caramelized.

Cook the sausage according to the package
directions.

Spread the mustard onto each sausage, top each
with an even amount of the caramelized onions
and a dollop of jam.

CALORIES: 560.3; TOTAL FAT: 36.6g; SODIUM: 317.4mg; TOTAL
CARBOHYDRATES: 39.2g; DIETARY FIBER: 8.2g; SUGARS: 3.4g;
PROTEIN: 18.9g

APPETIZERS AND SNACKS

Red Pepper Bisque
and Crabcake Shooters

These tasty, salty shooters are guaranteed to hit the spot.

Serves 4

....

½ onion, diced

½ carrot, diced

½ stalk celery, diced

1 tablespoon (15ml) olive oil

3 cups (700ml) vegan chicken broth or vegetable broth

1 cup (175g) diced roasted red peppers

¼ cup (56g) vegan cream cheese

Gardein mini crabless cakes (or homemade, see Tip below)

In a small pan with oil, cook the onions, carrots, and celery on medium-low heat until softened.

Place the cooked vegetables, broth, red peppers, and cream cheese in a blender. Blend until smooth, and add more broth if needed. Warm sauce up in a small saucepan.

Cook the crab cakes according to the package directions.

Place red pepper bisque in small shooter glasses. Cut a slice into each cake and place it onto the rim of each shooter glass.

CALORIES: 111.5; **TOTAL FAT:** 6.7g; **SODIUM:** 384mg; **TOTAL CARBOHYDRATES:** 9.3g; **DIETARY FIBER:** 2.7g; **SUGARS:** 3.1g; **PROTEIN:** 4.4g

HOMEMADE CRABLESS CAKES

Make your own meatless crab cakes! Squeeze out the liquid from the tofu, and then cook the tofu in fish stock for 15 minutes. Drain, dry, and coarsely chop it, and then mix it with cooked diced onion, garlic breadcrumbs, mayonnaise, mustard, and an egg substitute binder. Form into cakes and fry in a skillet with oil until brown and crispy on both sides and cooked through. Season with salt and pepper to taste.

Italian BLT Sliders

These mini-sammies pack loads of flavor in a small package thanks to the zippy rustic tomato vinaigrette.

Serves 4

12 ounces (340g) Impossible Meat

1 cup (113g) vegan mozzarella, shredded

4 mini vegan slider buns

2 ounces (57g) frisée lettuce

2 cups (475ml) rustic tomato vinaigrette (see page 135 for the Stuffed Italian Sub with Rustic Tomato Vinaigrette for instructions)

Make four 3-ounce (85g) mini sliders with the meat and cook per package directions. Melt the cheese on top of each slider.

Place the burgers onto the bottom halves of the buns and top with the lettuce, the rustic tomato vinaigrette, and the top halves of the buns.

CALORIES: 337.9; TOTAL FAT: 19g; SODIUM: 567.3mg; TOTAL CARBOHYDRATES: 24.7g; DIETARY FIBER: 3.1g; SUGARS: 3.1g; PROTEIN: 18g

Sausage Bread Sticks

All you need is a little puff pastry, cheese, and some Impossible Pork
to make savory bread sticks you'll start to crave all the time.

Serves 4

8 ounces (226g) Impossible
Pork

1 sheet puff pastry

1 cup (113g) vegan cheddar
cheese, shredded

1 tablespoon (15ml) olive oil

Preheat the oven to 400°F (200°C).

Crumble the pork into small pieces, and cook it
according to the package directions.

On a parchment-lined baking sheet, lay out the puff
pastry. Divide the cheese and cooked pork equally
and place onto the pastry. Cut the pastry into 1-inch
(2.5cm) slices, then twist each slice. Brush each pastry
twist with oil. Bake in the preheated oven for about 20
minutes or until the pastry is golden brown and crispy.

CALORIES: 333.1; TOTAL FAT: 22g; SODIUM: 381.7mg; TOTAL
CARBOHYDRATES: 21g; DIETARY FIBER: 2.4g; SUGARS: 0.5g; PROTEIN: 12.3g

Easy Cheeseburger Dip

A hearty game-day snack that's simple and delicious, this dip
is guaranteed to win over even the most die-hard meat fans.

Serves 4

8 ounces (226g) Beyond Meat Beyond
Beef Crumbles, Beefy

1½ cups (462g) vegan cheese sauce

¼ cup (60g) salsa

2 tablespoons (30ml) relish

12-ounce (340g) bag vegan corn or
potato chips

Cook the beef crumbles according to the
package directions.

Warm the cheese sauce in a small
saucepan on medium-low heat.

Place the warmed cheese, salsa, relish,
and cooked beef into a serving bowl and
serve with chips.

CALORIES: 591.8; **TOTAL FAT:** 33.6g; **SODIUM:** 753.8mg;
TOTAL CARBOHYDRATES: 63.4g; **DIETARY FIBER:** 5.9g;
SUGARS: 6.7g; **PROTEIN:** 10.9g

Figs and Pigs in a Blanket

A savory-sweet pairing that always feels right, these little piggies can be found at the market in the vegan aisle.

Serves 4–6

9 ounces (255g) Gardein Sliced Italian Saus'age

1 sheet of filo dough

8 figs, cut in half

2 tablespoons (30ml) olive oil

1 tablespoon (15ml) sea salt

1 teaspoon pepper

3 tablespoons (45ml) honey

¼ cup (60ml) vegan Dijon-style mustard

3 tablespoons (45ml) hot sauce

Preheat the oven to 400°F (200°C).

Cook the sausage according to the package directions.

Cut the filo sheet into 1-inch (2.5cm) strips, and then cut strips in half.

Place a piece of the sausage and a fig-half together on a strip of dough and roll it up. Place it on a baking sheet lined with parchment paper that has been brushed with oil. Continue to roll the remaining fig and pig blankets. Brush the tops of the dough with oil and sprinkle with sea salt and pepper.

Bake for 15–20 minutes or until the dough is lightly browned and cooked through.

Mix together the honey, mustard, and hot sauce in a small bowl. Serve with Fig and Pigs in a Blanket.

CALORIES: 283; TOTAL FAT: 6.8g; SODIUM: 519.6mg; TOTAL CARBOHYDRATES: 44.5g; DIETARY FIBER: 3.5g; SUGARS: 17.3g; PROTEIN: 11.7g

Corn Dog Bites

A school-lunch classic gets a modern update courtesy of
a smaller portion and Beyond Meat's spicy Italian sausages.

Serves 4

14 ounces (397g) Beyond Meat Beyond Sausage, Hot Italian

1 cup (128g) yellow cornmeal

1 cup (128g) unbleached flour

¼ teaspoon salt

⅛ teaspoon black pepper

¼ cup (50g) coconut sugar

4 teaspoons baking powder

4 tablespoons (28g) arrowroot flour

1 cup (240ml) almond milk

Oil for frying

Cook the sausage according to the package directions. Cut each sausage into 3 equal pieces.

In a medium-size bowl, mix together the cornmeal, flour, salt, pepper, sugar, baking powder, and arrowroot flour. Stir in the almond milk.

In a heavy-bottomed pan, add oil and preheat to 350°F (180°C), making sure you have enough oil to cover the sausage (about 1½–2 inches [4–5 cm]).

Place each sausage piece onto a skewer and dip in the batter to coat the sausages.

Fry the sausage skewers until the batter reaches a golden-brown color. Fry in batches so you don't overcrowd the pan.

CALORIES: 467.8; TOTAL FAT: 14.2g; SODIUM: 797.1mg; TOTAL CARBOHYDRATES: 62.4g; DIETARY FIBER: 8.8g; SUGARS: 8.2g; PROTEIN: 22.8g

Beef Crostini with Horseradish Sauce

Save this recipe for the next time you're hosting a get-together.

Serves 6–8

Vegan Steak

2 cups (304g) vital wheat gluten

¼ cup (22g) chickpea flour

2 tablespoons (30ml) vegan beef base broth powder

¼ cup (56g) tomato paste

1 teaspoon beet powder

1 tablespoon (15ml) vegan steak sauce, plus ¼ cup (60ml) for coating later in the recipe

½ teaspoon onion powder

¼ cup (60ml) olive oil

½ teaspoon black pepper

Crostini

French bread

1 clove garlic, peeled

Horseradish Sauce

1 cup (240g) vegan sour cream

2 tablespoons (30ml) lemon juice

3 tablespoons (45ml) prepared horseradish

½ teaspoon black pepper

½ teaspoon salt

Fresh herbs, for garnish

In a medium-size bowl, mix together all the vegan steak ingredients. Knead the dough to ensure the equal distribution of all ingredients. Form the dough into a London broil shape (approximately a 6 × 9 × 2-inch rectangle).

In a large Dutch oven with a lid, bring enough water to cover the steak by 1 inch (approximately 4 quarts of water depending on the size of your Dutch oven) to a boil. Gently add the steak and lower the heat to a soft simmer. Cover and cook for 2 hours or until the internal temperature reaches 180°F (80°C), turning once during cooking.

Preheat the oven to 350°F (180°C).

Cut the bread into ¼-inch (6mm) slices. Place in the oven and toast to a golden brown on both sides. Remove and rub garlic over each crostini. Set aside.

Mix the horseradish ingredients together in a small bowl.

Place the steak sauce in a shallow dish. Remove the steak from the water and place the steak into the sauce. Turn the steak, so it absorbs sauce on all sides.

In a nonstick frying pan over medium heat, brown the steak on all sides.

Slice the steak on a thin diagonal cut, as you would for a London broil.

Place a slice or two of steak onto a prepared crostini and top with horseradish sauce and fresh herbs, if using.

CALORIES: 165.3; TOTAL FAT: 4.1g; SODIUM: 194.8mg; TOTAL CARBOHYDRATES: 12.4g; DIETARY FIBER: 1.1g; SUGARS: 3.5g; PROTEIN: 18.5g

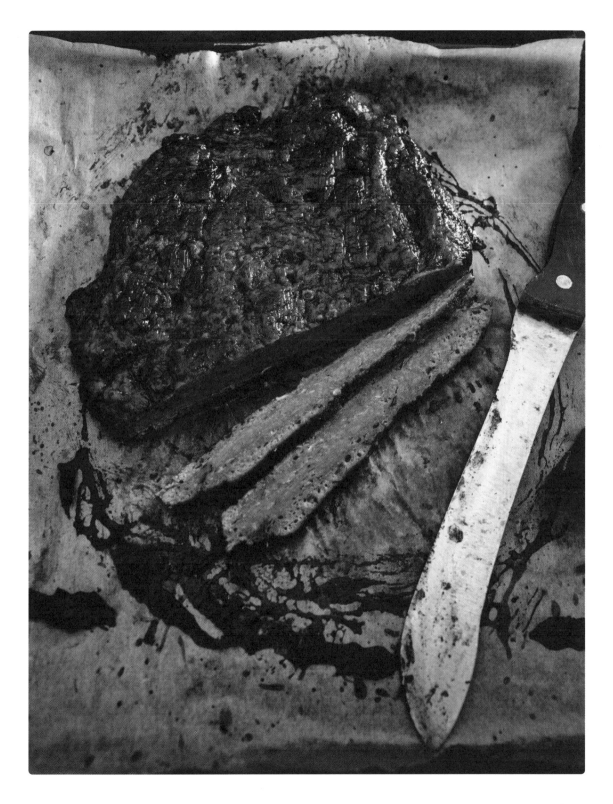

Jalapeño, White Bean, and Chicken Cheese Dip

This zesty starter has as much flavor as its non-plant-based equivalent, with none of the guilt.

Serves 4

16 ounces (454g) firm tofu

2 tablespoons (30ml) vegan chicken base powder

1 tablespoon (15ml) olive oil

1 can small white beans, drained

1 cup (240g) vegan sour cream

1 cup (225g) vegan cream cheese

1 cup (240ml) vegan mayonnaise

1 cup (113g) vegan shredded cheddar cheese

1 cup (113g) vegan mozzarella cheese

6 jalapeños, seeded and finely diced

Parsley (optional)

Preheat the oven to 400°F (200°C).

Place the tofu in a cheesecloth or clean kitchen towel and squeeze the liquid from the tofu.

In a medium-size bowl, break up the tofu and mix in the chicken base. Grease a parchment-lined baking sheet with oil and place the mixture on it. Bake in the preheated oven for about 40 minutes, stirring twice during cooking.

In a baking dish, mix together the white beans, sour cream, cream cheese, mayonnaise, cheeses, and jalapeños. Mix in the cooked tofu mixture.

Place a baking dish in the oven and bake for 15-20 minutes or until the mixture starts to bubble around the edges and is slightly browned on top. Garnish with chopped parsley, if desired, and serve with vegan chips or crackers.

CALORIES: 477.3; TOTAL FAT: 40.5g; SODIUM: 1,047.5mg; TOTAL CARBOHYDRATES: 17.4g; DIETARY FIBER: 4.6g; SUGARS: 1.1g; PROTEIN: 8.2g

Tofu Beef Jerky

Make this chewy, invigorating favorite before your next hike,
ball game, or road trip for stress-free snacking.

Serves 4–6

1 pound (454g) extra-firm tofu

2 tablespoons (30ml) vegan
beef-flavored soup base

2 teaspoons vegan steak sauce

¼ cup (60ml) low-sodium
soy sauce

¼ cup (60ml) water

⅛ teaspoon liquid smoke

Gently press the tofu to squeeze out the liquid.
Slice into ½-inch (12mm) thick strips

Mix the remaining ingredients together in a
shallow 13 × 9-inch (33 × 23-cm) baking dish.
Place the tofu into the baking dish in a single layer.
Let it soak overnight in the refrigerator.

Drain the excess liquid. Place the tofu in a food
dehydrator or 200°F (90°C) oven. This will take
6-8 hours. Flip the tofu over every hour to dry it
evenly. Dehydrate the jerky until it is very chewy
and all the white has disappeared.

CALORIES: 67.0; **TOTAL FAT:** 3.7g; **SODIUM:** 376.7mg; **TOTAL
CARBOHYDRATES:** 2.4g; **DIETARY FIBER:** 0.7g; **SUGARS:** 0.9g;
PROTEIN: 7.2g

Pasta Salad Skewers

All the flavors of the Mediterranean in a simple, shareable skewer make these the perfect snack for any occasion.

Serves 4

4 links Field Roast Italian Sausage

32 cooked vegan medium pasta shells

16 prepared artichoke hearts

16 grape tomatoes

¼ cup (60ml) vegan Italian dressing

¼ cup (28g) vegan Parmesan cheese

Cook the sausage according to the package directions. Slice into 16 even slices.

Using 16 small appetizer-size skewers, place a pasta shell, sausage slice, artichoke heart, tomato, and another pasta shell onto each skewer. Drizzle with dressing and sprinkle with Parmesan cheese.

CALORIES: 285.3; **TOTAL FAT:** 11.5g; **SODIUM:** 521.7mg; **TOTAL CARBOHYDRATES:** 26.2g; **DIETARY FIBER:** 3.3g; **SUGARS:** 1.3g; **PROTEIN:** 17.5g

Herb Pepper Jelly Dip with Sausage

Fresh herbs are the way to go for this satisfying
spread that's sure to wow your guests.

Serves 4

1 cup (225g) vegan cream cheese

1 teaspoon fresh chopped parsley

1 teaspoon fresh chopped basil

¼ teaspoon fresh chopped rosemary

½ cup (162g) vegan pepper jelly

4 links Field Roast Italian Sausage

Mix the cream cheese with the parsley, basil, and rosemary.

Place the cream cheese mixture into a small serving bowl and top with the pepper jelly.

Cook the sausage according to the package directions for the grill. Slice the cooked sausage into ½-inch (12mm) rounds and serve with the dip.

CALORIES: 315.2; TOTAL FAT: 21.2g; SODIUM: 715.3mg; TOTAL CARBOHYDRATES: 17.3g; DIETARY FIBER: 6.1g; SUGARS: 7.5g; PROTEIN: 16g

Santa Fe Stuffed Jalapeño Poppers

These southwest show-stoppers pack a perfect
combination of flavors into every bite.

Serves 4

5 ounces (142g) Beyond Meat Beyond
Beef Crumbles, Feisty

½ cup (56g) shredded vegan cheddar
cheese

¼ cup (60g) vegan salsa

8 large jalapeño peppers

¼ cup (60g) vegan sour cream

1 small bunch cilantro, chopped

2 tablespoons (6g) green onions,
chopped (optional)

Preheat the oven to 425°F (220°C).

Cook the beef crumbles according to the
package directions.

In a large bowl, mix together the cooked beef
crumbles, cheese, and salsa.

Cut the jalapeños in half, scoop out the seeds,
and spoon the meat mixture into each pepper
half.

Place the stuffed jalapeños onto a parchment-
lined baking sheet and cook in the preheated
oven for about 10-12 minutes.

Take out of the oven and garnish with a dollop
of sour cream, cilantro, and green onions, if
desired.

CALORIES: 191.7; TOTAL FAT: 12g; SODIUM: 549mg; TOTAL
CARBOHYDRATES: 11.7g; DIETARY FIBER: 2.3g; SUGARS: 2.3g;
PROTEIN: 9.1g

Sausage Bites

Caramelized onions and blackberry jam help
build layers of flavor in these delicious treats.

Serves 4

2 tablespoons olive oil

2 onions, sliced

9 ounces (255g) Gardein Sliced
Italian Saus'age

¼ cup (60g) spicy brown mustard

¼ cup (60g) vegan blackberry jam
(or your favorite flavor)

In a nonstick skillet over low heat, add the oil and
cook the onions, stirring often, until brown and
caramelized.

Cook the sausage according to the package
directions.

Spread the mustard onto each sausage and top
each with an equal amount of caramelized onions
and a dollop of jam.

CALORIES: 560.3; TOTAL FAT: 36.6g; SODIUM: 317.4mg; TOTAL
CARBOHYDRATES: 39.2g; DIETARY FIBER: 8.2g; SUGARS: 3.4g;
PROTEIN: 18.9g

Loaded Twice-Baked Sweet Potatoes

Twice-baked potatoes always hit the mark, and that goes double for these Impossible Pork–laden sweets.

Serves 4

4 small sweet potatoes

5 ounces (142g) Impossible Pork

½ cup (56g) shredded vegan cheddar cheese

¼ cup (56g) vegan cream cheese

2 tablespoons (6g) chopped fresh chives

Preheat the oven to 350°F (180°C).

Wash the sweet potatoes and spear with a fork. Place on a parchment-lined baking sheet and cook in the preheated oven for about 30 minutes or until tender. Remove from the oven and let them sit until cool enough to handle. Cut each in half lengthwise and scoop out the sweet potatoes, leaving ¼ inch (6mm) intact around the skin.

Cook the pork according to the package directions.

In a medium-size bowl, mix together the scooped out sweet potatoes, cooked pork, cream cheese, and cheddar cheese.

Fill the skins with the mixture. Return them to the oven until they are heated through and the cheese has melted. Remove from the oven and top with chives.

CALORIES: 190.3; TOTAL FAT: 9.4g; SODIUM: 362.1mg; TOTAL CARBOHYDRATES: 19.2g; DIETARY FIBER: 4.6g; SUGARS: 4.4g; PROTEIN: 8g

Deli Style Pinwheels

Just like you might find at your favorite corner store,
these colorful bites are as appealing to your eye
as they are satisfying to your appetite.

Serves 4

4 vegan tortillas

½ cup (132g) vegan hummus

8 Field Roast Lentil Sage
Deli Slices

3 ounces (85g) fresh spinach

8 Field Roast Garden Herb
Chao Slices

⅓ cup (40g) red pepper
bruschetta

Spread an equal amount of the hummus on each tortilla, place 2 slices of Lentil Sage Deli onto each, and top each with an equal amount of spinach, 2 slices of Garden Herb Chao, and bruschetta.

Roll the tortillas jelly-roll style. Cut into one-inch (2.5cm) rounds.

CALORIES: 992.2; TOTAL FAT: 61.3g; SODIUM: 1,185mg; TOTAL CARBOHYDRATES: 76.9g; DIETARY FIBER: 11.4g; SUGARS: 4.2g; PROTEIN: 31.4g

Stuffed Buffalo Meatballs

With a rich, flaming-hot flavor and a burst of melty cheese,
these Buffalo-style beef bites are an instant classic.

Serves 4–6

1 tablespoon (15ml) olive oil, plus more for frying meatballs

½ onion, diced

2 cloves garlic, minced

1 chia egg (1 tablespoon [15ml] chia seeds plus 2½ tablespoons [37ml] water)

12 ounces (340g) Impossible Burger

1 cup (90g) vegan seasoned panko breadcrumbs, divided

8 ounces (226g) shredded vegan mozzarella cheese

½ cup (120ml) vegan Buffalo sauce

¼ cup (60ml) vegan blue cheese dressing

¼ cup (6g) celery leaves, chopped

In a small pan over low heat, add oil and cook the onions and garlic until tender.

Mix together the chia egg and let it sit for 5 minutes.

In a medium-size bowl, mix together the meat, cooked onion mixture, chia egg, and ¼ cup of the breadcrumbs.

Make one-inch (2.5cm) round mini meatballs and stuff each meatball with a small piece of cheese. Roll the meatballs in the remaining breadcrumbs to coat.

In a large skillet over medium-high heat, add oil and cook the meatballs until browned on all sides and cooked through. Dip each meatball into buffalo sauce and drizzle with blue cheese dressing. Garnish with celery.

CALORIES: 118.6; TOTAL FAT: 4.6g; SODIUM: 569.1mg; TOTAL CARBOHYDRATES: 15.6g; DIETARY FIBER: 1.3g; SUGARS: 3g; PROTEIN: 3.7g

Pork and Coconut Dumplings

Enjoy island paradise authenticity without having to worry about the spit roast.

Serves 6–8

- 10 ounces (283g) Impossible Pork
- 1 tablespoon (15ml) olive oil
- ½ red pepper, finely diced
- ½ small onion, finely diced
- 1 clove garlic, minced
- 2 teaspoons curry powder
- 1 teaspoon ground coriander
- ½ teaspoon ground cinnamon
- 1 teaspoon crushed red pepper flakes
- ½ cup (120ml) coconut milk
- ¼ cup (41g) pineapple, diced
- 1 cup (200g) cooked rice
- 20–22 coconut wraps
- 2 green onions, chopped
- ¼ cup (31g) peanuts, chopped

Cook the pork according to the package directions.

In a small pan over medium heat, add the oil and cook the red pepper, onions, and garlic until softened.

In a large bowl, mix together the pepper mixture, pork, curry, coriander, cinnamon, red pepper flakes, coconut milk, pineapple, and cooked rice.

Place a tablespoon of the mixture into each of the wrappers and pinch the sides together to make a cup, leaving the top open.

In a large pan or skillet with a lid, over medium-high heat, add ⅛-inch (3mm) of water, and cook the dumplings for 5–7 minutes, covered. Check the pan and add more water if necessary.

Garnish with green onions and peanuts.

CALORIES: 175.7; **TOTAL FAT:** 11.3g; **SODIUM:** 135.9mg; **TOTAL CARBOHYDRATES:** 13.6g; **DIETARY FIBER:** 3.8g; **SUGARS:** 4.1g; **PROTEIN:** 6.6g

Feisty Stuffed Mushrooms

Button mushrooms are the perfect vessel for
the classic pairing of beef, onions, and peppers.

Serves 6–8

6 ounces (170g) Beyond Meat Beyond Beef Crumbles, Feisty

2 tablespoons (30ml) olive oil

1 small onion, finely diced

2 cloves garlic, minced

½ red pepper, diced

½ teaspoon cumin

½ teaspoon cayenne pepper

1 cup (60g) cooked black beans, chopped

½ cup (45g) vegan seasoned breadcrumbs

¾ cup (180ml) vegan beef broth

24 button mushrooms

Preheat the oven to 375°F (190°C).

Cook the beef crumbles according to the package directions.

In a large skillet over medium-low heat, add the oil and cook the onions, garlic, red pepper, cumin, and cayenne until the vegetables are tender.

In a large bowl, mix together the cooked beef, cooked onion mixture, beans, breadcrumbs, and broth.

Remove the stems from the mushrooms and brush the mushrooms clean with a damp cloth or paper towel.

Stuff each mushroom with a scoop of the meat filling. Place on a parchment paper-lined baking sheet. Cook the mushrooms until tender (about 20–30 minutes).

CALORIES: 152.9; TOTAL FAT: 3.9g; SODIUM: 416.0mg; TOTAL CARBOHYDRATES: 20g; DIETARY FIBER: 4.1g; SUGARS: 2.9g; PROTEIN: 10.2g

Pastry Paté Bites

These silky smooth, flaky appetizers will leave your guests wondering where you went to culinary school.

Serves 6–8

1 sheet of puff pastry

¼ cup olive oil plus 2 tablespoons (90ml)

8 ounces (226g) Beyond Meat Beyond Beef, Ground

½ cup (34g) baby bella mushrooms, diced

½ small onion, small diced

1 small clove garlic, minced

¼ teaspoon dried thyme, crushed

¼ teaspoon salt

¼ teaspoon pepper

¼ cup (28g) balsamic pearls

Preheat the oven to 400°F (200°C).

Cut the pastry into 1½-inch (38mm) squares. Place the pastry squares on a baking sheet lined with parchment paper. Brush the tops of the squares with 1 tablespoon (15ml) olive oil and place in a preheated oven. Cook for about 15 minutes or until lightly browned and crispy. Set aside.

Cook the ground beef according to the package directions.

In a small frying pan over medium-low heat, add 1 tablespoon (15ml) oil and cook the mushrooms, onions, and garlic until the ingredients are softened.

In a food processor, mix together the cooked beef, mushrooms, onion, garlic, thyme, salt, and pepper. Stream in the remaining ¼ cup olive oil until the mixture becomes a smooth spreadable consistency.

Place the pastries onto a serving plate, top with the desired amount of paté, and top each with balsamic pearls.

CALORIES: 218.5; TOTAL FAT: 15.2g; SODIUM: 129.0mg; TOTAL CARBOHYDRATES: 15.7g; DIETARY FIBER: 1g; SUGARS: 0.6g; PROTEIN: 5.2g

BBQ Sausage Bites

These tasty mini-meatballs will satisfy your guests by the handful.

Serves 4–6

....

1½ cups (350ml) vegan tomato sauce

¼ cup (60ml) apple cider vinegar

¼ cup (60ml) pure maple syrup

2 tablespoons (25g) coconut sugar

1 tablespoon (15ml) dry mustard

1 tablespoon (15ml) hot sauce

1 teaspoon chili powder

1 teaspoon paprika

1 teaspoon onion powder

1 teaspoon garlic powder

4 links Beyond Meat Beyond Sausage, Hot Italian

Place all the ingredients, except the sausage, in a medium saucepan and bring to a simmer on medium-low heat. Cook for about 10–15 minutes or until reduced and thickened.

Cook the sausage according to the package directions. Slice into ½-inch (12mm) pieces. Add to the sauce and serve with toothpicks.

CALORIES: 211; TOTAL FAT: 8.8g; SODIUM: 520.6mg; TOTAL CARBOHYDRATES: 22.5g; DIETARY FIBER: 3.6g; SUGARS: 12.8g; PROTEIN: 11g

Charcuterie Skewers

Perfect for a pre-meal spread, particularly if you're short on time, these skewers come together with very little fuss.

Serves 4–6

3 links Field Roast Italian Sausage

8 ounces (226g) vegan cheese

½ English cucumber

1 red pepper, cut into bite-size pieces

8 black or green olives, pitted

1 pint (300g) grape tomatoes

Small bunch fresh basil leaves

½ cup (120ml) vegan Italian dressing

Cook the sausage according to the package directions. Cut into ½-inch (12mm) slices.

Cut the cheese into ½-inch (12mm) cubes. Cut the cucumber in half, remove the seeds, and cut into ½-inch (12mm) slices.

Cut the peppers into bite-size pieces.

With mini skewers, place sausage, cheese, tomato, cucumber, pepper, olive, and basil onto skewers. Drizzle with dressing.

CALORIES: 168.8; **TOTAL FAT:** 12.5g; **SODIUM:** 394.2mg; **TOTAL CARBOHYDRATES:** 8.1g; **DIETARY FIBER:** 1.5g; **SUGARS:** 2.4g; **PROTEIN:** 5.8g

Rice Balls

An exceptional snack or starter, these rice balls are great
for dunking in tomato sauce or your favorite dressing or dip!

Serves 4

Flax egg (2½ tablespoons [37ml] ground flaxseed plus 5 tablespoons [75ml] warm water)

8 ounces (226g) Impossible Meat

3 cups (600g) cooked white rice, cooled

¾ cup (81g) vegan mozzarella cheese, shredded

1 teaspoon dried basil

1 cup (90g) vegan breadcrumbs

3 tablespoons (33g) nutritional yeast flakes

2 cups (475ml) vegan tomato sauce

Oil for frying

To make the flax egg, mix the flaxseed and water together in a small bowl and let sit for about five minutes.

Cook the beef according to the package directions.

In a large bowl, mix together the cooked beef, flax egg, rice, cheese, and basil.

In a shallow bowl, mix together the breadcrumbs and nutritional yeast.

With wet hands, form golf ball-size balls with the rice mixture. Coat each rice ball with the breadcrumb mixture. Place on a parchment-lined sheet pan and place in the refrigerator for about an hour.

Fill a heavy-bottomed pan with about half an inch of oil. Heat the oil to 360°F (180°C) and fry the rice balls on both sides until golden brown. Drain on a paper towel.

In a small saucepan over low heat, warm the sauce. Serve the sauce on the side, for dipping.

CALORIES: 519.3; TOTAL FAT: 22.4g; SODIUM: 582.8mg; TOTAL CARBOHYDRATES: 62.9g; DIETARY FIBER: 5.6g; SUGARS: 1.8g; PROTEIN: 20.5g

Szechuan Beef Skewers

You can back the heat off these tasty skewers by going easy
on the cayenne, or double it if you're feeling bold.

Serves 4–6

½ cup (112g) sesame tahini

1 clove garlic

4 tablespoons (60ml) freshly
squeezed lemon juice

2–6 tablespoons (30–90ml)
water

½ teaspoon salt

⅛ teaspoon cayenne

10.6 ounces (300g) Gardein
Szechuan beefless strips

1 tablespoon (15ml) sesame
seeds, toasted

2 green onions, chopped

Place the tahini, garlic, lemon juice, water, salt, and
cayenne pepper into a blender and blend to a smooth
consistency. Add more water if needed.

Cook the beef according to the package directions.
Place the cooked meat on skewers, drizzle with sauce,
and garnish with sesame seeds and green onions.

CALORIES: 595; TOTAL FAT: 38.4g; SODIUM: 284.4mg; TOTAL
CARBOHYDRATES: 39.7g; DIETARY FIBER: 7.4g; SUGARS: 3.6g; PROTEIN:
12.5g

Sausage and Grilled Pear Crostini

If you're not already a fan of this combination, you'll be delighted to learn how perfectly pork and pear pair up.

Serves 4

Vegan French bread

1 9-oz (256g) package Gardein Sliced Italian Saus'age

1 pear, cored and sliced

12 fresh sage leaves

1 tablespoon (15ml) olive oil

¼ cup (60g) vegan sour cream

Preheat the oven to 350°F (180°C).

Cut the French bread into twelve ½-inch (12mm) rounds. Place on a baking sheet and toast lightly on both sides in the oven. Set aside.

Cook the sausage according to the package directions. Place the pear slices on a well-greased, hot grill and cook until grill marks are achieved.

In a small pan on low heat, fry the sage leaves in olive oil until browned and crispy. Place on a paper towel to absorb any excess oil.

Place a grilled pear slice onto each crostini and top with a slice of sausage, a dollop of sour cream, and a fried sage leaf.

CALORIES: 317.6; TOTAL FAT: 8.9g; SODIUM: 665mg; TOTAL CARBOHYDRATES: 36.5g; DIETARY FIBER: 3.6g; SUGARS: 5g; PROTEIN: 13.5g

SOUPS, SALADS, AND SIDES

Apple Cranberry and Sausage Stuffing

This stuffing is bursting with flavor and
makes any meal feel like a special occasion.

Serves 4

3 links Field Roast Smoked Apple Sage Sausage

2 tablespoons (30ml) olive oil, divided

2 stalks celery, diced

1 medium onion, diced

2 sweet apples, cored and chopped

10 cups (16 ounces) (454g) vegan stuffing mix (or your own seasoned, toasted bread cubes)

1 cup (120g) dried cranberries

¼ teaspoon dried rosemary

½ teaspoon dried thyme

½ teaspoon dried sage

2 cups (475ml) low-sodium vegetable broth

Preheat the oven to 375°F (190°C).

Cook the sausage according to the package directions. Chop the cooked sausage and set it aside.

In a medium skillet over medium heat, add 1 tablespoon (15ml) oil and cook the celery, onions, and apples until tender, about 8 minutes.

Brush an oven-safe baking dish with the remaining oil.

In a large bowl, mix together the stuffing mix, onion mixture, cranberries, rosemary, thyme, sage, and broth.

Place the mixture into the greased baking dish and cook in the preheated oven for 20 minutes, covered. Uncover and cook for another 10 minutes or until the top of the stuffing is slightly browned.

CALORIES: 406.9; **TOTAL FAT:** 10.9g; **SODIUM:** 1,020.5mg; **TOTAL CARBOHYDRATES:** 40.2g; **DIETARY FIBER:** 5.9g; **SUGARS:** 10.4g; **PROTEIN:** 23.5g

Southwest Hasselback Sweet Potato Bake

These insta-worthy potatoes look as good as they taste and have an added savory layer courtesy of the Feisty crumbles.

Serves 4

4 sweet potatoes

5 ounces (142g) Beyond Meat Beyond Beef Crumbles, Feisty

½ cup (30g) black beans, cooked

½ cup (100g) diced tomatoes

4 Field Roast Tomato Cayenne Chao Slices

Preheat the oven to 375°F (190°C).

Wash the sweet potatoes and pierce each several times with a fork. Place on a tray. Place the tray in the oven and bake for 30–40 minutes or until just tender.

Cook the beef crumbles according to the package directions.

Place the sweet potatoes in an oven-safe baking dish. Cut a ½-inch slice into each sweet potato. Open the slices slightly and fill with the beef crumbles, beans, and tomatoes. Top each with a slice of the Tomato Cayenne Chao.

Return to the oven and continue to bake until the sweet potatoes are tender and the cheese has melted.

CALORIES: 194.1; TOTAL FAT: 7.5g; SODIUM: 426.3mg; TOTAL CARBOHYDRATES: 23.5g; DIETARY FIBER: 5.1g; SUGARS: 4.5g; PROTEIN: 8.2g

Tofu Pho

This rich, Vietnamese-style soup is a true winter warmer. To scale back the spice, be sure to remove the jalapeño seeds.

Serves 4

6 cups (1.5 liters) vegetable stock

1 1-inch (2.5cm) piece fresh ginger, peeled

1 tablespoon (15ml) olive oil

1 pound (454g) extra firm tofu, drained, pressed, and cut into ½-inch cubes

8 ounces (226g) rice noodles

7 ounces (198g) enoki mushroom, cleaned

3 green onions, green parts only

3 cups (327g) chopped napa cabbage leaves

2 carrots, julienned

2 jalapeño peppers, sliced

Sesame oil

Lime wedges (optional)

In a large soup pot over medium-high heat, add the stock and ginger and bring to simmer for 15–20 minutes. Remove the ginger.

In a medium nonstick frying pan over medium-high heat, add the oil and cook the tofu until lightly browned on all sides.

Cook the rice noodles according to the package directions. Drain and rinse the noodles.

Divide the mushrooms, onions, cabbage, carrots, cooked tofu, and rice noodles equally into 4 serving bowls. Fill each bowl with broth, and then garnish with jalapeño, sesame oil, and limes, if desired.

CALORIES: 431.9; **TOTAL FAT:** 8.3g; **SODIUM:** 81.4mg; **TOTAL CARBOHYDRATES:** 45.4g; **DIETARY FIBER:** 5.7g; **SUGARS:** 2.2g; **PROTEIN:** 15.7g

Cream of Potato and Sausage Soup

This rib-sticking soup is all you'll want to eat once the weather gets colder.

Serves 4

2 tablespoons (30ml) olive oil

1 medium onion, chopped

2 stalks celery, diced

1 large carrot, diced

2 cloves garlic, minced

1 teaspoon salt

½ teaspoon ground black pepper

4 tablespoons (32g) all-purpose flour

2 cups (475ml) non-dairy milk

3 cups (700ml) vegetable broth

5 medium potatoes, cut into ½- to ¾-inch (12mm to 24mm) pieces

10 ounces (283g) Impossible Pork

In a large soup pot over medium-high heat, add the oil and cook the onions, celery, and carrots until tender (about 5–8 minutes). Add the garlic, salt, and pepper and cook another minute. Mix the flour into the pot and cook, stirring, for a couple of minutes. Slowly whisk in the milk, continue to whisk until thickened, then whisk in the broth slowly. Add the diced potatoes. Bring to a soft simmer and continue to cook until the potatoes are tender.

Break up the pork into small pieces and cook according to the package directions.

Place the soup into the bowls and top with cooked sausage.

CALORIES: 396.7; **TOTAL FAT:** 8.5g; **SODIUM:** 755.4mg; **TOTAL CARBOHYDRATES:** 60.2g; **DIETARY FIBER:** 10.5g; **SUGARS:** 6.5g; **PROTEIN:** 21.5

Tofu Tots

A snacky side the whole family can agree on, these faux tots have a satisfying crunch of fried panko that helps them taste like the real deal.

Serves 4

16 ounces (454g) firm tofu

¼ cup (32g) cornmeal

½ cup (42g) panko

½ teaspoon onion powder

¼ teaspoon garlic powder

¼ teaspoon dried parsley

¼ teaspoon dried basil

¼ teaspoon salt

¼ teaspoon black pepper

½ tablespoon nutritional yeast

oil for frying

½ cup (120ml) vegan ketchup

Press as much liquid from the tofu as possible. Cut into Tater Tot–size pieces.

In a medium-size bowl, mix together the cornmeal, panko, onion powder, garlic powder, parsley, basil, salt, pepper, and nutritional yeast.

Press the tofu pieces into the panko mixture to coat all sides.

In a heavy-bottomed pan with ½ inch (12mm) of oil, heated to 360°F (180°C), fry the tots until golden brown on all sides. Drain on a paper towel. Serve with ketchup.

CALORIES: 132.8; **TOTAL FAT** 3.5G; **SODIUM:** 139.7mg; **TOTAL CARBOHYDRATES:** 20.8g; **DIETARY FIBER:** 2.5g; **SUGARS:** 0.9g; **PROTEIN:** 7.1g

Chopped Teriyaki Chicken Salad

The light but flavorful pineapple vinaigrette would be the star of this salad if Gardein's Teriyaki Chick'n Strips weren't so delicious.

Serves 4

10.5 ounces (298g) Gardein Teriyaki Chick'n Strips

1 large bunch fresh kale, chopped

¼ cup (50g) diced roasted beets

¼ cup (43g) red pepper, diced

½ cup (50g) diced purple cabbage

2 green onions, chopped

1 tablespoon sesame seeds

Pineapple Vinaigrette

½ cup (82g) chopped fresh pineapple

¼ cup (60ml) apple cider vinegar

1½ teaspoons toasted sesame oil

½ cup (120ml) olive oil

1 teaspoon freshly grated ginger

¼ teaspoon salt

¼ teaspoon pepper

Cook the chicken strips according to the package directions.

Place all the salad ingredients except the sesame seeds into a serving platter or bowl, top with the prepared chicken, and garnish with the sesame seeds.

Place all the salad dressing ingredients in a blender and blend until smooth. Serve the salad dressing alongside the salad.

CALORIES: 195; **TOTAL FAT 9.9G; SODIUM:** 306.4mg; **TOTAL CARBOHYDRATES:** 11.7g; **DIETARY FIBER:** 4.5g; **SUGARS:** 3.3g; **PROTEIN:** 16.7g

Mexican Street Corn

This traditional south of the border snack gets an upgrade courtesy of Beyond Meat's Feisty crumbles.

Serves 4

10 ounces (283g) Beyond Meat Beyond Beef Crumbles, Feisty

4 cups (660g) corn, fresh or frozen

½ large red pepper, diced

2 fresh jalapeño peppers, seeded and diced

¼ cup (60g) vegan salsa

4 oz (113g) vegan cream cheese

¼ teaspoon paprika

1 cup (113g) shredded vegan cheddar cheese

Preheat the oven to 350°F (180°C).

Cook the beef crumbles according to the package directions.

In a medium-size bowl mix all ingredients. Transfer the mixture into an oven-safe baking dish.

Place in the preheated oven. Bake for 15–20 minutes or until hot and bubbly.

CALORIES: 351.7; **TOTAL FAT:** 17.9g; **SODIUM:** 942.6mg; **TOTAL CARBOHYDRATES:** 35.3g; **DIETARY FIBER:** 8.7g; **SUGARS:** 10.4g; **PROTEIN:** 17.0g

Teriyaki Chinese Chicken Salad

Find your favorite soy sauce and break out your chopsticks because this salad is as good as anything from your favorite take-out joint.

Serves 4–6

....

10.5 ounces (298g) Gardein Teriyaki Chick'n Strips

5 cups (375g) chopped romaine lettuce

1 cup (75g) shredded red cabbage

⅓ cup (30g) grated carrots

2 tablespoons (30ml) rice wine vinegar

1 clove garlic, minced

1 tablespoon (15ml) sesame oil

½ tablespoon (12g) coconut sugar

½ teaspoon grated fresh ginger

1 teaspoon low sodium soy sauce

1 tablespoon (15ml) sesame seeds, toasted

¼ cup (12g) vegan chow mein noodles

¼ cup (22g) slivered almonds, toasted

Cook the chicken strips according to the package directions.

On a large serving platter or in a large bowl add the lettuce, cabbage, and carrots.

In a container with a lid, add the vinegar, garlic, oil, sugar, ginger, soy sauce, and sesame seeds. Shake to combine.

Top the salad with the chicken, chow mein noodles, and almonds. Drizzle the dressing over the salad.

CALORIES: 92.2; **TOTAL FAT:** 5.7g; **SODIUM:** 111.2mg; **TOTAL CARBOHYDRATES:** 6.6g; **DIETARY FIBER:** 2.3g; **SUGARS:** 2.3g; **PROTEIN:** 4.9g

Easy Poutine

Skip the trip up north and make this
Canadian favorite in your own kitchen.

Serves 4

....

28 ounces (794g) frozen French
fries (your favorite brand)

8 ounces (226g) Impossible
Burger

4 teaspoons (20ml) vegan broth
base and seasoning

1 tablespoon (7g) cornstarch

1 cup (113g) vegan cheddar
cheese, shredded

Cook the French fries according to the package
directions.

Break up the burger meat and cook according
to the package directions.

In a small saucepan over medium heat, mix the
broth base and 2 cups (473ml) water and bring
to a simmer.

In a small bowl, mix together cornstarch with
1 tablespoon (15ml) water. Stir the mixture into
the simmering broth. Continue to simmer until
thickened. Stir in the cooked Impossible Burger.

Place the French fries into a serving bowl and top
with gravy and cheese.

CALORIES: 292.4; TOTAL FAT: 13.5g; SODIUM: 738.4mg; TOTAL
CARBOHYDRATES: 38.3g; DIETARY FIBER: 4.2g; SUGARS: 0g;
PROTEIN: 5g

Creamy Smoked Apple-Sausage Soup

Reminiscent of a Buffalo-wings-style dip, this rich, spicy
soup brightens up any cold winter day.

Serves 4

- 10 ounces (283g) Field Roast Smoked Apple Sage Sausage
- 2 tablespoons (30ml) olive oil, divided
- 1 small onion, diced
- 1 stalk celery, diced
- 2 carrots, diced
- 3 tablespoons (32g) unbleached all-purpose flour
- 2 cups (475ml) non-dairy milk
- 4 cups (950ml) low sodium vegetable broth
- 8 ounces (226g) vegan cream cheese
- ¼ cup (60ml) hot sauce, more if desired

Cook the Field Roast Smoked Apple Sage Sausage according to the package directions. Cut the sausage into ½-inch (1.25cm) slices.

In a large soup pot over medium high heat, add 1 tablespoon (15ml) oil and cook the onion, celery, and carrots until softened.

Add the remaining oil and flour to the soup pot. Whisk in the milk and broth and cook for an additional 2 minutes. Stir in the cream cheese.

Simmer for 15 minutes or until the broth is reduced and thickened. Stir in the hot sauce and cooked sliced sausage.

CALORIES: 375.0; **TOTAL FAT:** 19.4g; **SODIUM:** 1,104.0mg; **TOTAL CARBOHYDRATE:** 23.2g; **DIETARY FIBER:** 6.6g; **SUGARS:** 6.7g; **PROTEIN:** 28.3g

Feisty Beef and Rice Soup

All your favorite homestyle flavors come together in this hearty
dish. You can even sub cauliflower rice for the white rice.

Serves 4

1 tablespoon olive oil

1 small onion, diced

1 large carrot, diced

1 stalk celery, diced

5 cups (1.25 liters) prepared
vegan beef-flavored broth
base

2 cups (475ml) vegan tomato
sauce

2 cups (330g) fresh or frozen
corn kernels

1 10-ounce (296ml) can diced
tomatoes and green chilies

10 ounces (283g) Beyond
Meat Beyond Beef
Crumbles, Feisty

2 cups (400g) cooked white
rice

1 cup (113g) vegan cheddar
cheese, shredded
(optional)

In a large soup pot over medium heat, add the oil and
cook the onions, carrots, and celery until softened. Add
the broth, sauce, corn, and diced tomatoes and green
chilies. Simmer the soup for 15 minutes.

Meanwhile, cook the beef crumbles according to the
package directions.

Add the cooked beef crumbles and rice to the soup.
Garnish with cheese, if desired.

CALORIES: 347.0; TOTAL FAT: 8.8g; SODIUM: 900.24mg; TOTAL
CARBOHYDRATES: 45.5g; DIETARY FIBER: 5.0g; SUGARS: 6.2g;
PROTEIN: 23.2g

Blackened Tofu Steak and Creamed Spinach

No reservations needed for this steakhouse standard, and the classic spinach side has a hit of heat and loads of flavor.

Serves 4

16 ounces (454g) firm tofu

2 tablespoons (30ml) blackening seasoning

3 tablespoons (45ml) olive oil, divided

1 medium onion, sliced

2 cloves garlic, minced

20 ounces (567g) baby spinach

½ cup (120ml) non-dairy milk

5 ounces (142g) vegan cream cheese

¼ teaspoon cayenne pepper

¼ teaspoon sea salt

¼ teaspoon black pepper

¼ cup (28g) vegan grated Parmesan

Drain the tofu, squeezing out as much liquid as possible. Cut into bite-size pieces and coat with the blackening seasoning.

In a large nonstick frying pan over medium-high heat, add 2 tablespoons (30ml) oil and fry the tofu until lightly browned on all sides. Drain on a paper towel.

In the same pan, add the remaining oil and cook the onions until softened. Add the garlic and continue to cook another minute. Add in the spinach and cook down, stirring often. Stir in the milk, cream cheese, cayenne, salt, pepper, and Parmesan cheese. Place the cooked spinach onto a serving plate and top with the tofu.

CALORIES: 204.1; TOTAL FAT: 11.7g; SODIUM: 423.7mg; TOTAL CARBOHYDRATES: 12.4g; DIETARY FIBER: 6.1g; SUGARS: 2g; PROTEIN: 14.3g

Lobster Salad

Treat yourself to the most delicious flavors of the sea
with this summertime favorite.

Serves 4

16 ounces (454g) firm tofu

1 stalk celery, diced

2 green onions, chopped

1 teaspoon finely diced nori

1 tablespoon (15ml) fresh lemon
juice

1 teaspoon Old Bay seasoning

¼ teaspoon white pepper

¼ teaspoon paprika

⅓ cup (30ml) vegan mayonnaise

12 leaves Boston lettuce

Place the tofu in a cheesecloth or clean kitchen towel and squeeze as much liquid from the tofu as possible. Break up into small pieces resembling chopped lobster into a medium-size bowl. Mix in the celery, onions, nori, lemon juice, Old Bay seasoning, pepper, paprika, and mayonnaise.

Line a serving dish with the lettuce and top with the lobster salad.

CALORIES: 163.6; TOTAL FAT: 11.3g; SODIUM: 207.6mg; TOTAL CARBOHYDRATES: 6.3g; DIETARY FIBER: 2g; SUGARS: 2.7g; PROTEIN: 12.2g

Vietnamese Noodle Salad with Tofu

Perfect as an opening course or full meal, this authentic Asian dish is worth the effort.

Serves 4

1 cup (240ml) mushroom broth

¼ cup (60ml) rice vinegar

1 tablespoon (15ml) fish sauce

3 teaspoons (15ml) coconut sugar

1 medium clove garlic, minced

½ teaspoon sea salt

¼ teaspoon crushed red pepper flakes

16 ounces (454g) firm tofu

1 tablespoon (15ml) olive oil

12 ounces (340g) white vermicelli rice noodles, cooked

4 cups (400g) sliced romaine lettuce

2 carrots, grated

½ English cucumber, sliced in half lengthwise, seeded, and sliced

1 cup (100g) bean sprouts

1 lime, cut into wedges

1 green onion, sliced on a diagonal

¼ cup (31g) chopped roasted peanuts

In a large shallow baking dish mix together the broth, vinegar, fish sauce, coconut sugar, garlic, salt, and pepper flakes. With a cheesecloth or clean kitchen towel, carefully squeeze as much moisture out of the tofu without it breaking apart. Slice the tofu into ½-inch (12mm) slices. Place the slices into the baking dish in a single layer. Refrigerate for 4–6 hours or overnight.

Heat the oil in a nonstick pan on medium-high heat. Take the tofu out of the marinade, and place it in the hot oil. Cook the pieces on both sides until browned, cooking in batches to avoid overcrowding the pan.

Arrange the vermicelli, lettuce, carrots, cucumbers, and bean sprouts around the serving platter. Place the tofu in the middle, tuck the lime wedges into the salad, and garnish with the green onions and peanuts. Serve with your favorite peanut, sesame, or Vietnamese dressing.

CALORIES: 322.9; TOTAL FAT: 13.9g; SODIUM: 586.1mg; TOTAL CARBOHYDRATES: 39g; DIETARY FIBER: 5.7g; SUGARS: 8.3g; PROTEIN: 16.8g

Smashed New Potatoes with Mexican Style Cheese Sauce

A little heat from the Field Roast sausage takes these cheese-covered potatoes to another level.

Serves 4

2 pounds (1kg) small red or gold potatoes

1 tablespoon (15ml) olive oil

2 links Field Roast Mexican Chipotle Sausage

1 cup (268g) vegan cheese sauce

¼ cup (60g) vegan salsa

Preheat the oven to 350°F (180°C).

Wash the potatoes and place them on a parchment-lined baking sheet. Drizzle with the oil and mix to coat. Bake the potatoes for about 15–20 minutes or until soft. Take out of the oven and smash each potato with a metal measuring cup just enough to flatten but not crush it. Increase the heat to broil, place the potatoes back in the oven, and bake until the tops are golden brown and crispy.

Meanwhile, cook the sausage according to the package directions. Cut into small pieces.

In a small saucepan over low heat, add the cheese sauce and heat until warm. Stir in the salsa and cooked sausage pieces.

Place the cooked potatoes onto a serving platter and top with cheese sauce.

CALORIES: 460.5; **TOTAL FAT:** 29.7g; **SODIUM:** 584.8mg; **TOTAL CARBOHYDRATES:** 36g; **DIETARY FIBER:** 2.8g; **SUGARS:** 1.6g; **PROTEIN:** 17.2g

Pomegranate, Apple, and Sausage Salad with Clementine Dressing

The bright citrus and light fruit blends incredibly well with the Impossible Pork for a simple salad that can easily be an entree.

Serves 4

10 ounces (283g) Impossible Pork

2 apples, cored and sliced

1 tablespoon (15ml) lemon juice

5 cups (375g) mixed greens

½ cup pomegranate seeds

¼ cup (60ml) freshly squeezed clementine juice

2 tablespoons (30ml) white balsamic vinegar

1 tablespoon (15ml) Dijon mustard

1 tablespoon (15ml) Bee Free Honee® or maple syrup

⅛ teaspoon black pepper

Break the sausage into small pieces and cook according to the package directions.

Coat the sliced apples with lemon juice to prevent the apples from turning brown.

Place the lettuce on a platter and top with the cooked pork, apples, and pomegranate seeds.

Place the clementine juice, vinegar, mustard, honey, and black pepper into a small container with a lid. Shake to combine the ingredients and serve with the salad.

CALORIES: 263; TOTAL FAT: 9.2g; SODIUM: 285.7mg; TOTAL CARBOHYDRATES: 31g; DIETARY FIBER: 6.4g; SUGARS: 20.4g; PROTEIN: 13.3g

Roasted Acorn Squash and Sausage Bits

Sometimes the ingredients do all the hard work for you, as
in this straightforward side dish with loads of flavor.

Serves 4

1 acorn squash

1 small red onion, sliced

1 tablespoon (15ml) olive oil

¼ teaspoon sea salt

¼ teaspoon black pepper

8 ounces (226g) Impossible Sausage

¼ cup (44g) pomegranate seeds

Preheat the oven to 375°F (190°C).

Wash the squash and cut it in half. Scoop out
the seeds. Cut each half into ½-inch (12mm)
slices.

Place the squash and onions on a parchment
paper-lined sheet pan, drizzle with oil, season
with salt and pepper, and toss to coat. Cook
for about 20 minutes or until the squash has
softened.

Meanwhile, cook the sausage according to the
package directions, breaking the sausage into
small pieces.

Place the cooked squash and onions on a
serving dish and top with cooked sausage
and pomegranate seeds.

CALORIES: 278; TOTAL FAT: 8.7g; SODIUM: 679mg; TOTAL
CARBOHYDRATES: 41.9g; DIETARY FIBER: 12g; SUGARS: 4.9g;
PROTEIN: 12.5g

Wild Mushroom and Potato Stacks

These two-bite potato stacks are loaded with rich umami flavor and also have an undeniable aesthetic appeal.

Serves 4

4 medium potatoes

5.5 ounces (156g) Field Roast Wild Mushroom Deli Slices

½ cup (120ml) vegan mayonnaise

1 small bunch fresh thyme leaves

If your muffin tins are not heavy metal pans, fill empty cups with water so the tin won't warp during cooking.

Preheat the oven to 375°F (190°C).

Slice the potatoes into thin rounds. Cut the Deli Slices the same size as the potatoes.

In a 12-cup muffin tin or two 6-cup muffin tins, brush eight of the cups with mayonnaise. Place two slices of potatoes, each brushed with mayonnaise, into the cups. Continue layering in the same manner until eight muffin cups are filled. Add a couple of thyme leaves into each stack while stacking.

Place the potato stacks into the preheated oven and cook for 20–30 minutes or until the potatoes are tender.

CALORIES: 381.3; TOTAL FAT: 15g; SODIUM: 461.1mg; TOTAL CARBOHYDRATES: 42.2g; DIETARY FIBER: 7.6g; SUGARS: 4.2g; PROTEIN: 18.2g

Mexican Chipotle Green Beans

With just a little spicy sausage, these otherwise plain
veggies go from straightforward to spectacular.

Serves 4

1 pound (454g) trimmed haricots verts

2 links Field Roast Mexican Chipotle
Sausage

2 tablespoons (30ml) olive oil

3 tablespoons (18g) minced shallots

1 garlic clove, minced

⅛ teaspoon sea salt

⅛ teaspoon black pepper

¼ cup (32g) chopped toasted pecans

1 tablespoon (15ml) chopped fresh
parsley

Bring a large pot of water to a boil. Add the
green beans and cook for 3 minutes. Transfer
the beans to a bowl of ice water to stop the
cooking. Drain the beans and set aside.

In a large skillet, cook the sausage according
to the package directions. Remove it and cut it
into large dice. Set aside.

In the same skillet over medium heat, add the
oil and cook the shallots and garlic for about
2 minutes. Stir in the salt and pepper.

Return the cooked green beans to the skillet
and cook for about one minute. Top with
sausage, pecans, and parsley.

CALORIES: 153.2; TOTAL FAT: 7.1g; SODIUM: 335.5mg; TOTAL
CARBOHYDRATES: 8.7g; DIETARY FIBER: 2g; SUGARS: 2.7g;
PROTEIN: 14.6g

Chopped Chicken Waldorf Endive Salad

This New York classic still holds up and is better
than ever in this cruelty-free version.

Serves 4

10 ounces (283g) Gardein
  Chick'n Strips

2 stalks celery, chopped

2 apples, chopped

½ cup (65g) walnuts,
  chopped

1 cup (100g) grapes, chopped

½ cup (120ml) vegan avocado
  mayonnaise

16 endive leaves

Cook the chicken strips according to the package
directions. Chop chicken and set aside.

In a medium bowl, mix together the chopped chicken
strips, celery, apples, walnuts, grapes, and mayonnaise.

Wash and dry the endive leaves. Fill each endive with
an equal amount of salad.

CALORIES: 217.8; TOTAL FAT: 17.5g; SODIUM: 181.5mg; TOTAL
CARBOHYDRATES: 11.8g; DIETARY FIBER: 2.7g; SUGARS: 9.9g;
PROTEIN: 7.5g

Easy Pork Thai Curry Soup

With just three ingredients you can make
a soup that'll wow your whole family.

Serves 4

5 cups (1.25 liters) low sodium
vegetable broth

20-ounce (567g) package
Gardein Porkless Thai Curry

6.75 ounces (191g) rice noodles

In a soup pot over medium heat, heat the broth.

Cook the curry according to the package directions.

Add the cooked curry and noodles to the broth and
simmer for about 10 minutes or until the noodles
are tender.

CALORIES: 287.2; TOTAL FAT: 4.7g; SODIUM: 559.2mg; TOTAL
CARBOHYDRATES: 51.2g; DIETARY FIBER: 2.9g; SUGARS: 10.8g;
PROTEIN: 8.3g

Grilled Sausage and Pepper Potato Salad

Perfect for a picnic or potluck, this German-inspired
potato salad is a true crowd pleaser.

Serves 4

- 2 pounds (1kg) red potatoes, cut into bite-size pieces
- Oil for grilling
- 2 links Beyond Meat Beyond Sausage
- ¾ cup (180ml) vegan mayonnaise
- 1 tablespoon (15ml) Dijon-style mustard
- ¼ cup roasted red peppers, sliced
- 1 tablespoon (15ml) dried Italian seasoning

Place the potatoes in a large pot and fill with water to cover. Bring to a boil. Cook the potatoes until tender (about 20 minutes). Drain and cool in the refrigerator for about an hour.

On a hot greased grill, cook the sausage according to the package directions. Cut the cooked sausage on the diagonal into ½-inch (12mm) pieces. Set aside.

In a large bowl add the potatoes, sausage, mayonnaise, mustard, peppers, and Italian seasoning. Stir all the ingredients together.

CALORIES: 455.2; TOTAL FAT: 33.1g; SODIUM: 888.3mg; TOTAL CARBOHYDRATES: 25.4g; DIETARY FIBER: 4.6g; SUGARS: 2g; PROTEIN: 10.1g

Lemon Aioli and Crab Cake Salad

A delicious vegan aioli is the perfect complement to these flavorful crabless cakes.

Serves 4–6

1 cup (240ml) vegan mayonnaise

2 tablespoons (30ml) lemon zest

2 lemons, juiced

½ teaspoon white pepper

12 ounces (340g) Gardein Mini Crabless Cakes (or homemade, see page 40)

2 avocados, thinly sliced

2 cups (70g) assorted microgreen mixture

In a small bowl, mix together the mayonnaise, lemon zest, lemon juice, and pepper.

Cook the crab cakes according to the package directions.

On a serving platter, place a swish of the lemon aioli per crab cake. Place three slices of avocado onto the aioli swoosh. Top each with a cooked crab cake, another dollop of aioli, and some microgreens.

CALORIES: 576.1; **TOTAL FAT:** 46.8g; **SODIUM:** 480.2mg; **TOTAL CARBOHYDRATE:** 29.1g; **DIETARY FIBER:** 11.5g; **SUGARS:** 6.7g; **PROTEIN:** 11.2g

Spicy Seitan Pepperoni

Make your own pepper-faux-ni with this easy to follow recipe.

Serves 4

1½ cups (228g) vital wheat gluten

¼ cup (56g) tomato paste

1 teaspoon beet powder

¼ cup (60ml) low sodium vegan soy sauce

¼ cup (60ml) olive oil

1 teaspoon whole fennel seeds

1 tablespoon (15ml) garlic powder

1 tablespoon (15ml) smoked paprika

½ teaspoon black pepper

1 teaspoon crushed red pepper flakes

⅛ teaspoon liquid smoke

In a large bowl, mix together all the ingredients. Once the mixture starts to come together, finish mixing by hand. Knead the dough thoroughly to ensure even distribution of ingredients throughout the dough.

Place a steamer basket in a saucepan, add a couple of inches of water, and bring to a boil.

Divide the dough into two pieces and roll the dough into two logs about 5–6 inches (12–15cm) long.

Roll each log up loosely in a piece of aluminum foil, twisting the ends closed. Steam for 40 to 60 minutes.

Remove the pepperoni from the steamer and cool completely in the fridge. The pepperoni will swell while cooling.

Once cooled, remove from the foil, slice, and serve as an appetizer or use on pizzas, in pastas, or other favorite dishes.

CALORIES: 120.7; TOTAL FAT: 14.4g; SODIUM: 695mg; TOTAL CARBOHYDRATES: 6.9g; DIETARY FIBER: 1.1g; SUGARS: 0.1g; PROTEIN: 19.9g

Sausage Mac and Cheese

It's hard to argue with this comfort classic, and everyone will agree it's even better with a little Impossible Pork.

Serves 4

....

14 ounces (397g) vegan macaroni noodles

8 ounces (226g) Impossible Pork

4 tablespoons (60ml) olive oil

5 tablespoons (40g) unbleached all-purpose flour

2¼ cups (532ml) unsweetened non-dairy milk

1 cup (113g) vegan cheddar cheese, shredded

½ cup (56g) vegan Parmesan cheese

½ teaspoon salt

½ teaspoon black pepper

¼ teaspoon onion powder

1 tablespoon (15ml) Dijon-style mustard

4 tablespoons (45g) nutritional yeast

¼ cup (22g) vegan panko breadcrumbs

Preheat the oven to 350°F (180°C).

In a large pot of boiling salted water, cook the macaroni following the package directions for al dente.

Break the sausage up into small pieces. Cook according to the package directions.

Add the oil to a large saucepan on medium heat, add the flour, and whisk the flour and oil together, cooking for a couple of minutes. Slowly add the milk, whisking continually to thicken the sauce. Whisk in the cheeses, salt, pepper, onion powder, mustard, and nutritional yeast. If the sauce is not smooth, place it in a blender and blend until smooth, then add the cooked sausage.

Place the cooked pasta and cheese sauce together in an oven-safe baking dish. Top with panko breadcrumbs and cook in the preheated oven for about 30 minutes or until the mac and cheese is bubbling and the top is lightly golden brown. Serve immediately.

CALORIES: 558; TOTAL FAT: 17.8g; SODIUM: 604mg; TOTAL CARBOHYDRATES: 68.8g; DIETARY FIBER: 6.7g; SUGARS: 2.8g; PROTEIN: 27.1g

MAIN DISHES

Meatloaf Muffin Parmesan

This dish is a hearty meal in a handful-size package, and the chia egg adds authentic texture to this flavorful classic.

Serves 2–4

1 tablespoon (15ml) olive oil

1 tablespoon (15ml) chia seeds

3 tablespoons (45ml) water

16 ounces (454g) Beyond Beef Plant-Based Ground

⅓ cup (44g) onion, finely chopped

¼ cup (44g) red pepper, finely chopped

¼ cup (7g) spinach, finely chopped

½ cup (36g) mushroom, finely chopped

¼ teaspoon pink Himalayan salt

¼ teaspoon pepper

1 teaspoon dried parsley

½ teaspoon dried basil

½ teaspoon garlic powder

½ cup (120ml) vegan pasta sauce (your favorite brand, or homemade)

½ cup (65g) vegan mozzarella cheese, shredded

Grease 5 portions of a cupcake pan with olive oil.

Preheat the oven to 350°F (180°C).

In a small bowl mix together the chia seeds and water and set aside for 10 minutes or until the mixture becomes gelatinous (chia egg).

In a large bowl add all the ingredients (except the pasta sauce and cheese) and the chia egg. Mix together. Form 5 equal meatloaf balls and place one into each of the greased cups. Top each meatloaf ball with an equal amount of sauce.

Place in the preheated oven and cook until the internal temperature reaches 165°F (70°C). Top each meatloaf with the cheese and continue to cook until the cheese has melted.

CALORIES: 302; **TOTAL FAT:** 21g; **SODIUM:** 541.2mg; **TOTAL CARBOHYDRATES:** 8.2g; **DIETARY FIBER:** 4.3g; **SUGARS:** 2g; **PROTEIN:** 21.8g

Orange Beef Ravioli with Cranberry Sauce

By using Gardein's Orange Beefless Bowl as the main ingredient,
half the prep work on these tasty wontons is already done.

Serves 4

- 8.5 ounces (240g) Gardein Orange Beefless Bowl
- 16–20 wonton wrappers
- 1 tablespoon (15ml) olive oil
- ⅓ cup (32g) minced shallot
- 1 teaspoon finely chopped fresh sage
- ½ teaspoon finely chopped fresh rosemary
- 2 cups (200g) fresh cranberries
- 3 tablespoons (34g) vegan brown sugar
- 2 teaspoons balsamic vinegar
- 1½ cups (354ml) low sodium vegan beef broth
- ¼ teaspoon black pepper

Cook the beef bowl according to the package directions. Chop the cooked ingredients.

Fill half the wonton wrappers with a tablespoon of the beef bowl mixture, leaving the edges free of filling. Wet the edges with water and top with the remaining wrappers, making sure there are no air pockets inside, and press to adhere.

In a small saucepan with oil, cook the shallot for a minute on medium-low heat. Add the sage, rosemary, cranberries, sugar, vinegar, broth, and pepper and continue to simmer until sauce is thickened and cranberries are softened.

CALORIES: 194.2; TOTAL FAT: 2.6g; SODIUM: 500.2mg; TOTAL CARBOHYDRATES: 34.8g; DIETARY FIBER: 2.4g; SUGARS: 5.4g; PROTEIN: 7.6g

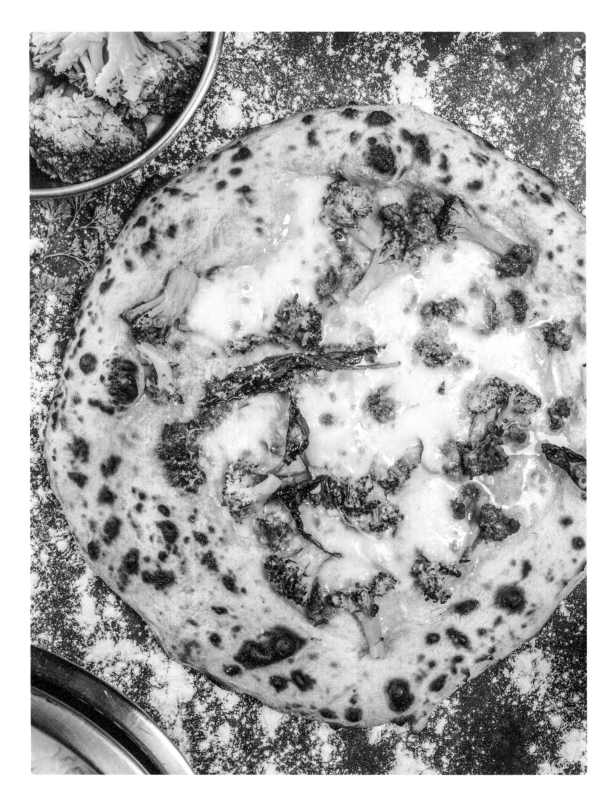

Beef and Broccoli Pizza

This crowd-pleasing pizza is so easy to make, the only thing
you'll need to worry about is who gets the last slice.

Serves 2–4

1 vegan ready-to-use
pizza crust, baked

8 ounces (226g)
Impossible Beef

¼ cup (60ml) low-sodium
soy sauce

1 tablespoon (12g)
coconut sugar

1 teaspoon minced fresh
ginger

2 cloves garlic, minced

⅓ cup (80ml) vegan
beef-flavored broth

½ tablespoon cornstarch

1 cup (113g) vegan
mozzarella cheese,
shredded

2 cups (142g) cooked
broccoli

1 tablespoon (15ml)
sesame seeds, toasted

Preheat the oven to 400°F (200°C).

Bake the pizza crust according to the package directions.

Break up the beef into bite-size pieces and cook according
to the package directions.

In a small saucepan on medium-low heat, add the soy
sauce, coconut sugar, ginger, garlic, and broth. Simmer
the sauce to reduce, stirring often (about 5 minutes). Stir
the cornstarch and ½ tablespoon (7ml) water together in
a small bowl. Add the cornstarch slurry to the simmering
sauce to thicken.

Place the cheese evenly on top of the prepared pizza
crust. Top the pizza evenly with the cooked beef and
broccoli. Drizzle with the sauce and place in the preheated
oven. Bake until the cheese has melted. Garnish with
sesame seeds.

CALORIES: 291; TOTAL FAT: 12.2g; SODIUM: 1,107.8mg; TOTAL CARBOHYDRATES:
47.6g; DIETARY FIBER: 3.5g; SUGARS: 2.9g; PROTEIN: 13.5g

Beef Stroganoff Stuffed Shells

Filling and flavorful, these shells might be all you need to sate your appetite.

Serves 4–6

1 pound (454g) large vegan pasta shells

10 ounces (283g) Beyond Meat Beyond Beef Crumbles, Beefy

4 tablespoons (60ml) olive oil, divided

1 onion, diced

1 pint (150g) baby bella mushrooms, cleaned, stemmed, and diced

¼ teaspoon dried thyme

2 tablespoons (16g) unbleached all-purpose flour

3 cups (700ml) vegan beef broth

½ cup (120g) vegan sour cream

2 cups (226g) shredded vegan mozzarella cheese, divided

Preheat the oven to 350°F (180°C).

Cook the shells according to the package directions for just under al dente. Drain.

Cook the beef crumbles according to the package directions.

In a medium-size pan with 1 tablespoon (15ml) oil, cook the onions, mushrooms, and thyme on medium heat until softened. Remove from the pan.

In the same pan, on medium heat, stir in the remaining oil and flour, cook for a minute or two, stirring often, and slowly whisk in the broth and sour cream to thicken.

In a medium-size bowl, mix together the cooked beef crumbles, 1 cup (113g) of cheese, and the mushroom mixture. Fill each shell with the mixture.

Place the stuffed shells in a large oven-safe baking dish, pour the sauce over the shells and into the baking dish, and top with the remaining cheese. Bake in the preheated oven for about 25 minutes or until bubbly and slightly browned on top.

CALORIES: 279.2; TOTAL FAT: 4.1g; SODIUM: 418.5mg; TOTAL CARBOHYDRATES: 49.3g; DIETARY FIBER: 3.3g; SUGARS: 1.9g; PROTEIN: 12.5g

Garlic and Oil Bucatini

These noodles are a great conduit for flavor, thanks to the hole that
makes them the perfect pasta for this peppery mustard sauce.

Serves 4

¾ pound (340g) vegan bucatini
or spaghetti

8 ounces (226g) Impossible Pork

¼ cup (22g) vegan seasoned
breadcrumbs

⅓ cup (80ml) olive oil

4 cloves garlic, minced

½ cup (120ml) low sodium vegan
chicken broth

1 teaspoon Dijon-style mustard

¼ teaspoon red pepper flakes

In a large pot of boiling salted water, cook the
pasta according to the package directions. Drain.

Crumble the pork into small pieces. Cook
according to the package directions.

In a small pan on low heat, toast the breadcrumbs,
stirring frequently, until lightly browned. Set aside.

In a large skillet with oil, cook the garlic for
1 minute on low heat. Add in the broth, mustard,
and red pepper flakes and bring to a simmer. Add
the cooked pork and cooked pasta to the skillet and
mix thoroughly. Add more broth if needed. Mix in
the toasted breadcrumbs to coat the pasta.

CALORIES: 573.9; **TOTAL FAT:** 21.9g; **SODIUM:** 571.4mg; **TOTAL
CARBOHYDRATES:** 73g; **DIETARY FIBER:** 4.8g; **SUGARS:** 2.8g;
PROTEIN: 22.1g

Country-Style Katsu Cutlets with Cherry Peppers

This delicious stovetop favorite from Japan benefits from a little spice, but you can use sweet peppers if that's your preference.

Serves 4–6

8 Field Roast Sunflower Country-Style Katsu Cutlets

1 tablespoon (15ml) olive oil

2 cups (180g) cherry peppers, sweet or hot or a combination, halved

¾ cup (180ml) cherry pepper pickling liquid

¾ cup (180ml) vegan chicken broth

2 tablespoons (14g) cornstarch

Cook the cutlets according to the package directions.

In a medium skillet over medium heat, add the oil and cook the peppers for a couple of minutes, stirring often. Stir in the cherry pepper pickling liquid and chicken broth. Bring the sauce to a simmer.

In a small bowl, mix the cornstarch with 2 tablespoons (30ml) of water. Whisk the cornstarch mixture into the simmering sauce and continue to simmer until thickened.

Place the cutlets on a platter and top with the cherry pepper sauce.

CALORIES: 360.1; **TOTAL FAT:** 11.3g; **SODIUM:** 843.1mg; **TOTAL CARBOHYDRATES:** 37g; **DIETARY FIBER:** 3.9g; **SUGARS:** 4.8g; **PROTEIN:** 26.6g

Easy Bolognese Sauce

Every good cook should be able to put together a classic Bolognese—
even the ones who cook without meat. Now you can!

Serves 4–6

1 stalk celery, shredded or finely chopped

1 small onion, shredded or finely chopped

1 carrot, shredded

2 cloves garlic, minced

2 tablespoons (30ml) olive oil

4 cups (1 liter) canned crushed tomatoes

1 tablespoon (15ml) dried basil

½ tablespoon dried parsley

1 teaspoon sea salt

1 teaspoon black pepper

8 ounces (226g) Impossible Beef

8 ounces (226g) Impossible Pork

¼ cup (56g) vegan cream cheese

In a large heavy-bottomed saucepan or Dutch oven, cook the celery, onions, and carrots in the oil on medium-low heat for 10–15 minutes or until lightly browned, stirring often. Stir in the tomatoes, basil, parsley, salt, and pepper. Bring the sauce to a simmer and cook for 20 minutes.

Break up the beef and pork into small crumbles and cook each according to the package directions.

Add the cooked beef and pork into the sauce. Stir in the cream cheese.

Serve with your favorite pasta.

CALORIES: 304.5; TOTAL FAT: 14.7g; SODIUM: 421.1mg; TOTAL CARBOHYDRATES: 23.5g; DIETARY FIBER: 6.6g; SUGARS: 8g; PROTEIN: 21.3g

Grilled Sausage with Mango Salsa

These Italian sausages grill as well as they pan-sear, allowing you to add a little flame-touched flavor to this island-inspired dish.

Serves 4

8 links Field Roast Italian Sausage

1 ripe mango, peeled and diced

½ cup (75g) cucumber, peeled, seeded, and diced

1 jalapeño, seeded and diced

½ red onion, diced

1 tablespoon (15ml) fresh lime juice

¼ teaspoon salt

¼ teaspoon pepper

4 cups (800g) cooked wild rice

Preheat a grill to medium heat.

Cook the sausage on the well-greased preheated grill according to the package directions.

In a medium-size bowl, mix together the mango, cucumber, jalapeño, onion, lime juice, salt, and pepper.

Place the rice on a platter, place the sausage on top of the rice, and add the mango salsa.

CALORIES: 440.5; TOTAL FAT: 10.7g; SODIUM: 576.5mg; TOTAL CARBOHYDRATE: 54.8g; DIETARY FIBER: 8.1g; SUGARS: 9.7g; PROTEIN: 32g

Creamy Chicken Scampi

Another revamped staple you can add to your repertoire, this dish subs out shrimp for tasty vegan chicken strips but keeps the lemony garlic sauce you love.

Serves 4

¾ pound (340g) vegan spaghetti or fettuccine

1 tablespoon (15ml) olive oil

3 cloves garlic, minced

1 cup (240ml) vegan chicken broth

¼ teaspoon red pepper flakes

1 teaspoon Dijon-style mustard

¼ cup (56g) vegan cream cheese

10 ounces (283g) Gardein Chick'n Strips

1 small lemon, juiced, plus zest of half the lemon

¼ cup (28g) vegan Parmesan cheese

2 tablespoons (30ml) chopped fresh parsley

In a large pot of salted boiling water, cook the pasta according to the package directions. Drain the pasta.

In a large skillet over medium heat, add the oil and cook the garlic for a minute or two (do not let garlic brown), stirring often. Add in the broth, red pepper flakes, mustard, and cream cheese. Continue to cook until the cream cheese is fully incorporated and the sauce has reduced and thickened.

Cook the chicken strips according to the package directions.

Place the cooked pasta and chicken into the skillet and stir to combine. Add more broth if needed. Remove from the heat and stir in the lemon juice and zest. Garnish with the Parmesan cheese and parsley.

CALORIES: 214.6; **TOTAL FAT:** 4.9g; **SODIUM:** 476.9mg; **TOTAL CARBOHYDRATES:** 29.3g; **DIETARY FIBER:** 2.6g; **SUGARS:** 1.3g; **PROTEIN:** 13.1g

Nacho Fries Topped Burger

For those nights when your hungriest guests are clamoring for something filling, serve up these burgers topped with even more protein.

Serves 4

4 Beyond Meat Beyond Burger patties

6 ounces (170g) Beyond Meat Beyond Beef Crumbles, Feisty

4 vegan burger buns

4 small servings of prepared vegan French fries

½ cup (100g) diced tomatoes

½ cup (75g) diced avocado

½ cup (112g) vegan cheese sauce

¼ cup (60g) vegan sour cream

Cook the burgers and the beef crumbles according to the package directions.

Split the burger buns and place the cooked burgers on the 4 bottoms. Top each burger equally with the fries, cooked beef crumbles, tomatoes, avocado, cheese sauce, and sour cream. Cover each with the top bun.

CALORIES: 589.5; TOTAL FAT: 28.4g; SODIUM: 882.9mg; TOTAL CARBOHYDRATES: 48.9g; DIETARY FIBER: 7.8g; SUGARS: 5.4g; PROTEIN: 35.2g

Brat Sausage Skillet Stew

This dish delivers layer after layer of delicious flavors, incorporating a rich broth with a subtle sweetness from apples and a nice zip from the mustard and faux brats.

Serves 4

6–8 links Beyond Meat Beyond Sausage, Brat Original

2 tablespoons (15ml) olive oil

1 large onion, sliced

2 pounds (1kg) fingerling (mini) potatoes, cut into bite-size pieces

¼ head purple cabbage, sliced thin

2 cups (200g) Brussels sprouts, trimmed and halved

¾ small sweet apple, julienned

3 cups (700ml) low sodium vegetable broth

1 tablespoon (15ml) grainy mustard

1 tablespoon (15ml) apple cider vinegar

½ teaspoon sea salt

½ teaspoon ground pepper

3 tablespoons (21g) cornstarch

2 tablespoons (30ml) fresh parsley, chopped

Cook the sausage according to the package directions. Slice the sausages or leave them whole for a more rustic look.

In a large skillet over medium heat, add the oil and cook the onions, potatoes, cabbage, Brussels sprouts, and the apple until the ingredients are slightly caramelized. Add in the broth, mustard, vinegar, salt, and pepper.

Place the sausage back into the skillet and simmer until the potatoes are tender (about 15–20 minutes). If the potatoes soak up too much broth, add more as needed.

Mix together the cornstarch and 3 tablespoons (45ml) of water in a small bowl. Stir it into the simmering broth to thicken the sauce. Garnish with parsley.

CALORIES: 493.6; **TOTAL FAT:** 19g; **SODIUM:** 909.2mg; **TOTAL CARBOHYDRATES:** 52.6g; **DIETARY FIBER:** 14g; **SUGARS:** 10.4g; **PROTEIN:** 31.2g

Crispy Spinach and Mushroom Wraps

Great for a meal on the go. Any time you need a delicious dish
in half the time, these wraps are tasty enough to savor.

Serves 4

4 tablespoons (60ml) olive oil

2 cups (56g) fresh spinach

¼ cup (60ml) vegan
mayonnaise

4 extra large vegan tortillas
(flatbread or lavash bread)

8 slices Field Roast Wild
Mushroom Deli Slices

8 slices Field Roast Garden
Herb Chao Slices

½ cup (88g) roasted red
pepper, sliced

¼ cup (60ml) vegan balsamic
syrup

In a frying pan over medium-high heat, add the oil and
fry the spinach in batches until crispy. Drain on a paper
towel. Set aside.

Spread the mayonnaise onto the tortillas. Top each with
the Wild Mushroom Deli Slices, crispy spinach, Garden
Herb Chao Slices, roasted red peppers, and a drizzle
of balsamic. Roll the tortillas halfway, fold the sides in,
and continue to roll.

CALORIES: 318.2; **TOTAL FAT:** 16.6g; **SODIUM:** 486.6mg; **TOTAL
CARBOHYDRATE:** 28.2g; **DIETARY FIBER:** 2g; **SUGARS:** 0.9g; **PROTEIN:** 6.1g

Lobster Club Sandwich

A little extra work goes a long way with these delicious faux-lobster sandwiches, which taste just as good for a fraction of the price.

Serves 4

16 ounces (454g) firm tofu

1 stalk celery, diced

2 green onions, chopped

1 teaspoon finely diced nori

1 tablespoon (15ml) fresh lemon juice

1 teaspoon Old Bay seasoning

¼ teaspoon white pepper

¼ teaspoon paprika

⅓ cup (80ml) vegan mayonnaise, extra for sandwiches

12 slices vegan bread

4 leaves lettuce

8 tomato slices

2 avocados, sliced

Place the tofu in a cheesecloth or clean kitchen towel and squeeze as much liquid from it as possible. Into a medium-sized bowl, break tofu into small pieces resembling picked lobster meat. Mix in the celery, onions, nori, lemon juice, Old Bay, pepper, paprika, and mayonnaise.

Place an equal amount of the lobster salad onto 4 slices of bread, top with another slice of bread, spread the mayonnaise onto the top of each bread slice, and add an equal amount of the lettuce, tomatoes, and avocados to each sandwich. Top each with the remaining bread slice.

CALORIES: 844.6; **TOTAL FAT:** 47.5g; **SODIUM:** 963.6mg; **TOTAL CARBOHYDRATES:** 66g; **DIETARY FIBER:** 16g; **SUGARS:** 11.5g; **PROTEIN:** 39.3g

Crab Cake Po-Boy with Avocado Mayonnaise

Take a trip to New Orleans without having to leave your backyard
with this vegan-friendly take on the Louisiana staple.

Serves 4

¾ cup (180ml) vegan mayonnaise

1 avocado, smashed with fork

2 tablespoons (30ml) fresh lemon juice

½ teaspoon black pepper

¼ teaspoon Old Bay seasoning

14 ounces (397g) Gardein Mini Crabless Cakes (or homemade, see page 40)

4 vegan hoagie rolls

2 cups (150g) chopped iceberg lettuce

12 slices ripe tomatoes

In a medium bowl, mix together the mayonnaise, smashed avocado, lemon juice, pepper, and Old Bay.

Cook the crab cakes according to the package directions.

Cut the rolls in half lengthwise. Place a generous amount of the avocado mayonnaise onto each roll, top each with the lettuce and tomatoes and cooked crab cakes.

CALORIES: 430.6; TOTAL FAT: 20.9g; SODIUM: 720.9mg; TOTAL CARBOHYDRATES: 51.3g; DIETARY FIBER: 5g; SUGARS: 6.1g; PROTEIN: 10.9g

Stuffed Italian Sub with Rustic Tomato Vinaigrette

A deli classic that never disappoints, these sandwiches are figuratively and literally overflowing with flavor.

Serves 4

1 pint (360g) cherry tomatoes, halved

3 tablespoons (45ml) olive oil

1 shallot, finely chopped

¼ cup (28g) sliced red onions

1 clove garlic, minced

1 tablespoon (15ml) white balsamic vinegar

1 teaspoon sea salt

½ teaspoon freshly ground pepper

1 large loaf vegan French bread

½ cup (120ml) vegan basil pesto

1 cup (75g) shredded iceberg lettuce

10 slices Field Roast Smoked Tomato Deli Slices

½ cup (88g) roasted red peppers, sliced

¼ cup (30g) peperoncini peppers, sliced

10 slices Field Roast Garden Herb Chao Slices

In a medium bowl, mix together the tomatoes, oil, shallots, onions, garlic, balsamic, salt, and pepper. Set aside.

Slice off the top third of the bread loaf. Scoop out the bread in the middle of the loaf, leaving ½ inch around the crust intact. Spread the pesto on the bottom of the loaf, top with the lettuce, Smoked Tomato Deli Slices, roasted red peppers, peperoncini peppers, and Garden Herb Chao Slices. Top with the tomato vinaigrette. Place the top back onto the loaf. Slice into 4 sandwiches.

CALORIES: 372.6; **TOTAL FAT:** 24.1g; **SODIUM:** 981.9mg; **TOTAL CARBOHYDRATES:** 22.8g; **DIETARY FIBER:** 3.4g; **SUGARS:** 2.1g; **PROTEIN:** 13.2g

Pepper Steaks with Mushrooms

A wild-west workhorse, these country-style steaks are made even better with the addition of your favorite mushrooms and a savory sauce.

Serves 4

2 tablespoons (30ml) olive oil

8 ounces (226g) crimini or porcini mushrooms, stemmed and halved

1 large onion, chopped

1 cup (240ml) vegan beef broth

¼ cup (56g) vegan cream cheese

½ teaspoon thyme, chopped

½ teaspoon parsley, chopped

¼ teaspoon rosemary, chopped

3 tablespoons (45ml) black peppercorns, cracked, divided

24 ounces (680g) Impossible Burger

In a large skillet over medium heat, add the oil and cook the mushrooms until browned. Add the onions and continue to cook until the onions are tender. Mix in the broth, cream cheese, thyme, parsley, rosemary, and 1 tablespoon (15ml) pepper. Simmer until the sauce is thickened.

Form the Impossible Burger into 4 steaks and season with the remaining 2 tablespoons (30ml) crushed pepper. Cook according to the package directions. Top with the sauce.

CALORIES: 432.4; **TOTAL FAT:** 24.7g; **SODIUM:** 737.4mg; **TOTAL CARBOHYDRATES:** 18.8g; **DIETARY FIBER:** 6.2g; **SUGARS:** 2.6g; **PROTEIN:** 31.6g

Chicken Pot Pie Bake

This "I can't believe it's not chicken" pot pie will have your guests thinking everything tastes like plant-based protein.

Serves 4–6

2 pounds (1kg) small white potatoes, halved

2 tablespoons (30ml) olive oil, divided

2 carrots, diced

1 small onion, diced

1 stalk celery, diced

⅓ cup (44g) corn kernels

1½ cups (354ml) vegan chicken broth

1 tablespoon (7g) cornstarch

10 ounces (283g) Gardein Chick'n Strips

½ cup (75g) peas, fresh or frozen

1 sheet of puff pastry

Preheat the oven to 400°F (200°C).

Place the potatoes in a large pot, fill with water, and bring to a boil. Cook the potatoes until fork tender (about 10–15 minutes). Drain.

In a medium skillet over medium-low heat, add 1 tablespoon (15ml) oil and cook the carrots, onions, celery, and corn until tender. Stir in the broth and bring to a simmer. In a small bowl mix together the cornstarch with 1 tablespoon water. Whisk into the simmering sauce to thicken.

Cook the chicken strips according to the package directions.

Place the sauce, cooked chicken strips, and peas into an oven-safe baking dish. Place the puff pastry on top of the mixture. Brush the top of the pastry with the remaining oil and place in the preheated oven. Cook for 12–15 minutes or until the puff pastry is lightly golden brown.

CALORIES: 337.6; TOTAL FAT: 12.9g; SODIUM: 763.8mg; TOTAL CARBOHYDRATES: 42.5g; DIETARY FIBER: 3.9g; SUGARS: 4.8g; PROTEIN: 12.3g

Roasted Squash and Sausage Risotto

Perfect for a fall dinner or winter brunch, this risotto lets the butternut squash take center stage (where it belongs!).

Serves 5

2½ cups (1.25 kg) diced butternut squash

3 tablespoons (45ml) olive oil, divided

¼ teaspoon sea salt

¼ teaspoon black pepper

12 ounces (340g) Impossible Pork

6 cups (1.5 liters) vegan low sodium chicken or vegetable broth

½ onion, diced

1 clove garlic, minced

2 cups (394g) arborio rice

1 cup (240ml) dry white wine

¼ cup (28g) finely grated vegan Parmesan, divided

2 tablespoons (30ml) chopped fresh parsley

Preheat the oven to 350°F (180°C).

Place the squash on a parchment-lined baking sheet, drizzle with 1 tablespoon (15ml) oil, and season with the salt and pepper. Toss to coat evenly and place in the preheated oven. Cook until the squash is tender (about 30–40 minutes). Remove from the oven and set aside.

Break up the pork and cook according to the package directions.

Warm the broth in a small saucepan.

In a nonstick or enamel skillet over medium-low heat, add the remaining oil and cook the onions and garlic for 3–4 minutes, until lightly browned. Add the rice, and lightly toast for about one minute, stirring often. Add the wine, and cook until the wine is fully absorbed.

Ladle enough broth to just cover the rice. Simmer the rice, stirring frequently, adding a ladle of broth at a time after each ladle of the broth has been absorbed. Cook until the rice has just become soft, with a slight bite in the middle of the grain.

Take the risotto off the heat, stir in the cooked pork, squash, Parmesan, and parsley.

CALORIES: 428; TOTAL FAT: 12.4g; SODIUM: 927mg; TOTAL CARBOHYDRATES: 53.8g; DIETARY FIBER: 8.7g; SUGARS: 3.5g; PROTEIN: 22.8g

Mexican Sloppy Joes

Beyond Meat's Feisty Crumbles bring the fiesta to these sandwiches, which are sure to become a welcome addition to your weekly rotation.

Serves 4

2 tablespoons (30ml) olive oil

½ onion, diced

2 cloves garlic, minced

1 tablespoon (8g) unbleached all-purpose flour

¾ cup (180ml) vegan beef broth

10 ounces (283g) Beyond Meat Beyond Beef Crumbles, Feisty

1 cup (60g) black beans, cooked

½ cup (88g) fresh or frozen corn

¼ cup (60ml) vegan ketchup

½ cup (120ml) vegan BBQ sauce

1 cup (113g) shredded vegan cheddar cheese

4–6 vegan sandwich buns

1 avocado, sliced

In a large nonstick skillet over medium-low heat, add the oil and cook the onions until tender. Add in the garlic and cook for another minute. Stir in the flour and cook for a minute or two. Whisk in the broth and continue to cook until thickened.

Cook the beef crumbles according to the package directions.

Place the cooked beef crumbles, beans, corn, ketchup, BBQ sauce, and cheddar cheese into the skillet and mix to combine.

Place an equal amount of filling onto 4 bottom buns, then top each with the avocado slices and the top buns.

CALORIES: 668.7; TOTAL FAT: 42.2g; SODIUM: 1,280.2mg; TOTAL CARBOHYDRATES: 74.3g; DIETARY FIBER: 10.2g; SUGARS: 13.1g; PROTEIN: 22.3g

Four-Ingredient Spaghetti and Meatballs

You'll be hard-pressed to find a simpler recipe in this or any cookbook. Since the pasta sauce is doing most of the work, feel free to splurge on your favorite or, better yet, make your own.

Serves 4

¾ pound (340g) vegan spaghetti

12.7 ounces (360g) Gardein Meatless Meatballs

2 cups (475ml) pasta sauce (your favorite brand or homemade)

¼ cup (28g) vegan Parmesan cheese

In a large pot of salted boiling water, cook the pasta according to the package directions.

Cook the meatballs according to the package directions.

In a large skillet over medium heat, add the sauce and heat through. Add in the pasta and meatballs to the sauce and stir to combine. Place on a serving dish and sprinkle with the Parmesan cheese.

CALORIES: 285.5; **TOTAL FAT:** 8.2g; **SODIUM:** 580.5mg; **TOTAL CARBOHYDRATES:** 35.6g; **DIETARY FIBER:** 6.3g; **SUGARS:** 4.4g; **PROTEIN:** 20.1g

Fish Filets with Lemon Cream Sauce and Asparagus

Describing a dish as having a light cream sauce feels like an oxymoron, but in this case it's accurate—and delicious.

Serves 4

1 pound (454g) fresh asparagus

2 tablespoons (30g) olive oil, divided

Salt and pepper, to taste

3 cloves garlic, minced

½ cup vegan (120ml) chicken broth

1 teaspoon oregano

2 tablespoons (28g) vegan cream cheese

1 lemon, zest and juice

14 ounces (397g) Gardein Golden Fishless Filet

1 tablespoon (15ml) chopped fresh parsley

Preheat the oven to 350°F (180°C).

Place the asparagus on a parchment paper-lined baking sheet. Drizzle with 1 tablespoon (15ml) oil and season with salt and pepper. Mix to coat. Bake in the preheated oven for about 10–12 minutes or until slightly charred and tender.

In a small skillet over medium-low heat, add the remaining oil and cook the garlic for a minute or so, stirring frequently. Stir in the broth, oregano, and cream cheese, then simmer to thicken the sauce. Take the sauce off the heat and stir in the lemon juice and lemon zest.

Cook the fish filets according to the package directions.

Place the roasted asparagus onto a serving platter, place the cooked fish filets on top, and pour the sauce over the top. Garnish with parsley.

CALORIES: 251.3; TOTAL FAT: 14.6g; SODIUM: 860mg; TOTAL CARBOHYDRATES: 20.7g; DIETARY FIBER: 7.1g; SUGARS: 2.1g; PROTEIN: 15.3g

Italian Style Beef Tips

One of the secrets to this dish is the homemade tomato vinaigrette. The other is that you didn't use actual beef.

Serves 4

2 cups (475ml) rustic tomato vinaigrette (see recipe for Stuffed Italian Sub with Rustic Tomato Vinaigrette, page 135, for instructions)

¼ cup (22g) vegan seasoned panko breadcrumbs

2 tablespoons (30ml) chopped fresh parsley

2 tablespoons (14g) vegan Parmesan cheese

1 tablespoon (15ml) lemon zest

2 9-ounce (255g) bags Gardein Beefless Tips

Pour vinaigrette into a medium skillet and cook on medium-low heat, stirring often, until the vegetables start to wilt and flavors meld (about 3-4 minutes).

In a small nonstick frying pan over low heat, toast the panko until light golden brown. Place in a small mixing bowl. Mix in the parsley, Parmesan, and lemon zest. Stir to combine. Set aside.

Cook the beef tips according to the package directions.

Place the tomatoes onto a serving dish, top with the cooked beef tips, and sprinkle with the breadcrumb mixture.

CALORIES: 226; **TOTAL FAT:** 7.1g; **SODIUM:** 815.8mg; **TOTAL CARBOHYDRATES:** 17.5g; **DIETARY FIBER:** 5g; **SUGARS:** 1.9g; **PROTEIN:** 25g

*This recipe can be served over rice.

Apple Sausage Grilled Cheese

"Apple sausage on grilled cheese?" you declare
incredulously before your life changes forever.

Serves 4

2 links Field Roast
Smoked Apple Sage
Sausage

8 slices Field Roast
Creamy Original Chao
Slices

8 slices vegan bread

1 cup (113g) vegan
cheddar cheese,
shredded

2 tablespoons (30ml)
olive oil or vegan
butter

Grill the sausages according to the package directions. Slice
into ¼-inch (6mm) rounds.

Place a slice of Chao on each of four slices of bread, top
each with an equal amount of sausage, an equal amount of
cheddar cheese, and another slice of the Chao. Place the
top slice of bread on each of the four sandwiches and brush
the top side with oil or butter.

Let a griddle or pan over medium heat get hot, then cook
the sandwiches, oil-side down until bread is golden brown,
flip to other side and grill until golden brown and cheese
has melted.

CALORIES: 384.1; TOTAL FAT: 18.4g; SODIUM: 899.7mg; TOTAL CARBOHYDRATES:
35.6g; DIETARY FIBER: 3.9g; SUGARS: 4.8g; PROTEIN: 18.6g

Scalloped Potatoes and Sausage Bake

Thinly sliced spuds and Field Roast Italian Sausage come together in this fantastic oven-baked classic.

Serves 4

2 pounds (1kg) baking potatoes

3 tablespoons (45ml) olive oil

1 clove garlic, minced

3 tablespoons (24g) unbleached all-purpose flour

2 cups (475ml) non-dairy milk

1 cup (240ml) low-sodium vegan chicken broth

2 cups (226g) vegan shredded cheddar cheese

1 teaspoon sea salt

½ teaspoon black pepper

3 links Field Roast Italian Sausage

Preheat the oven to 400°F (200°C).

Peel the potatoes and thinly slice or cut them with a mandoline into thin rounds.

In a medium-size pan over medium-low heat, add the oil and cook the garlic for a minute. Add in the flour and cook for another minute or two, stirring often. Slowly whisk in the milk and broth and simmer until thickened. Melt in the cheese and season with salt and pepper.

Cook the sausage according to the package directions. Slice into ¼-inch (6mm) slices.

In the bottom of an oven-safe baking dish, pour a ladleful of the sauce. Place a layer of the sliced potatoes, one-third of the sausage, and add another ladle of the sauce. Continue to layer ingredients in the same manner, finishing with a top layer of potatoes and sauce.

Place the baking dish in the preheated oven and bake for about 40 minutes or until bubbly and browned on top and the potatoes are tender.

CALORIES: 709.2; TOTAL FAT: 19.1g; SODIUM: 1,042mg; TOTAL CARBOHYDRATES: 84.8g; DIETARY FIBER: 15.1g; SUGARS: 9.6g; PROTEIN: 43.2g

Sausage Cacciatore Red Rice Bake

This incredibly tasty one-dish meal comes together in the oven,
freeing you up to focus on the rest of your to-do list.

Serves 4–6

14 ounces (397g) Beyond Meat
Beyond Sausage, Hot Italian

1 green pepper, diced

1 small onion, diced

1 clove garlic, minced

2 cups (475ml) tomato purée

3 cups (700ml) vegan chicken
broth

1 tablespoon (15ml) dried basil

½ teaspoon dried oregano

1 teaspoon sea salt

1 teaspoon black pepper

2 cups (370g) white rice

Preheat the oven to 350°F (180°C).

Cook the sausage according to the package
directions. Slice it into ½-inch (12mm) slices.

Place all the ingredients into an oven-safe baking
dish, including the sliced sausage. Cover with foil.

Place the baking dish into the preheated oven and
cook for about 30–40 minutes or until the rice is
tender.

CALORIES: 195.6; TOTAL FAT: 12.8g; SODIUM: 724.9mg; TOTAL
CARBOHYDRATES: 41.2g; DIETARY FIBER: 3.4g; SUGARS: 7.4g; PROTEIN:
5.3g

Steamed Tofu with Leeks

This stir-fry noodle dish could lean a little farther into the flavors of the east if you were inclined to add a little sesame oil or soy sauce.

Serves 4

8 ounces (226g) glass noodles

1 tablespoon (15ml) olive oil

2 leeks, sliced and cleaned

2 cloves garlic, minced

2 cups (475ml) vegan chicken broth or vegetable broth

½ teaspoon salt

½ teaspoon pepper

1 tablespoon (15ml) chopped fresh parsley

2 tablespoons (14g) cornstarch

16 ounces (454g) firm tofu

Cook the noodles according to the package directions.

In a medium skillet over medium-low heat, add the oil and cook the leeks for a couple of minutes, stirring often. Add in the garlic and cook for another minute. Stir in the broth and bring to a simmer. Season with the salt, pepper, and parsley. Mix the cornstarch with 2 tablespoons (30ml) water and whisk into the leeks to thicken the sauce.

Drain the tofu and cut it into 4 equal squares. Place in a steamer basket and steam for 5 minutes or until the tofu is warmed up.

Place the noodles on a platter, top with the steamed tofu, and pour the leek sauce on top.

CALORIES: 517.9; **TOTAL FAT:** 4g; **SODIUM:** 141.1mg; **TOTAL CARBOHYDRATES:** 28.4g; **DIETARY FIBER:** 1.6g; **SUGARS:** 1.3g; **PROTEIN:** 10.8g

Tofu Scallops

You can imbue your favorite tofu with the flavors of the sea by mixing it with finely diced kelp or nori—as in this seared faux scallop dish.

Serves 4

16 ounces (454g) firm tofu

1 teaspoon kelp flakes or nori, finely diced

1 teaspoon Old Bay seasoning

½ cup (64g) unbleached all-purpose flour

½ teaspoon salt

½ teaspoon pepper

3 tablespoons (45ml) oil for frying

Cut the tofu into 1½-inch (4cm) rounds. Place rounds on a paper towel and top with another paper towel to dry the "scallops."

In a shallow bowl, mix together the kelp, Old Bay, flour, salt, and pepper.

Coat the top and bottom of each scallop with the flour mixture.

In a large nonstick skillet over medium-high heat, add the oil and sear the scallops until golden brown on both sizes. Remove and drain on a paper towel.

CALORIES: 83.7; TOTAL FAT: 5.1g; SODIUM: 47.7mg; TOTAL CARBOHYDRATES: 6.3g; DIETARY FIBER: 0.6g; SUGARS: 0.3g; PROTEIN: 4.1g

*Scallops can be served with lemon aioli sauce, Asian sauce, or your favorite sauce.

Bang Bang Tofu Bowl

Two hits of spice from the sweet chili and hot sauces make
this eye-watering bowl worth the effort and the tears.

Serves 4

¾ cup (180ml) vegan mayonnaise

¼ cup (60ml) vegan sweet chili sauce

1 tablespoon (15ml) hot sauce

16 ounces (454g) firm tofu

¾ cup (84g) cornstarch

¼ teaspoon salt

¼ teaspoon pepper

1 teaspoon Old Bay seasoning

½ cup (120ml) vegan egg, not cooked

olive oil for frying

4 cups (800g) cooked rice

1 cup (75g) shredded iceberg lettuce

2 tablespoons (12g) chopped green onion

In a small bowl mix together the
mayonnaise, chili sauce, and hot sauce.
Set aside.

Drain the tofu and place in a cheesecloth
or clean kitchen towel and squeeze the
liquid from the tofu. Cut into bite-size
pieces.

In a shallow bowl mix together the
cornstarch, salt, pepper, and Old Bay.

Coat the tofu pieces with the egg, then
with the cornstarch mixture.

In a large, nonstick frying pan, heat
enough oil to fry the tofu to 350°F
(180°C). Carefully add the tofu and fry
until lightly golden brown on all sides.
Fry in batches to avoid overcrowding the
pan. Drain on a paper towel.

In a large bowl, toss together the cooked
tofu and the reserved sauce.

Divide the rice evenly into 4 bowls, top
with the lettuce, tofu (and sauce), and
green onion.

CALORIES: 742.8; **TOTAL FAT:** 45.2g; **SODIUM:**
1,006.3mg; **TOTAL CARBOHYDRATES:** 52.1g; **DIETARY
FIBER:** 3.6g; **SUGARS:** 1.4g; **PROTEIN:** 29.6g

BBQ Ribs

Ramp up your next backyard BBQ with these smoky, delicious "ribs." You'll be the envy of the neighborhood!

Serves 4

1½ (228g) cups vital wheat gluten (available at most health food stores or online)

¼ cup (56g) tomato paste

1 teaspoon beet powder

½ cup (120ml) vegan beef broth

1 teaspoon nutritional yeast

1 tablespoon (15ml) onion powder

½ teaspoon black pepper

8 craft sticks

¾ cup (180ml) vegan BBQ sauce

Preheat the oven to 375°F (190°C).

Preheat a grill or grill pan to medium heat.

In a large bowl, mix together the vital wheat gluten, tomato paste, beet powder, beef broth, nutritional yeast, onion powder, and pepper. Finish the mixing by hand. Knead the dough thoroughly to ensure even distribution of ingredients. Form the dough around each of the Popsicle sticks, creating flat rectangular shapes, each about 4 inches long and ¾ inch thick. Place the ribs on a well-greased hot grill and let grill marks form on the ribs.

Place the grilled ribs on a parchment-lined baking sheet. Place in the preheated oven and bake for 40 minutes or until the internal temperature reaches 180°F (80°C). Brush the ribs with BBQ sauce and place under the broiler to caramelize the sauce. Take the ribs out of the oven and brush with more BBQ sauce.

CALORIES: 68.2; TOTAL FAT: 0.5g; SODIUM: 476mg; TOTAL CARBOHYDRATES: 14.1g; DIETARY FIBER: 2.2g; SUGARS: 8g; PROTEIN: 3.9g

Spaghetti Pie

The Beyond Meat Beefy Crumbles are just one
of the stars of this Midwestern staple.

Serves 4–6

¾ pound (340g) vegan
spaghetti

10 ounces (283g) Beyond
Meat Beyond Beef
Crumbles, Beefy

1 tablespoon (15ml) olive oil

1 small onion, diced

2 cloves garlic, minced

1 tablespoon (15ml) chopped
fresh basil

1 cup (240ml) pasta sauce,
your favorite

½ cup (124g) vegan ricotta
cheese

½ cup (56g) vegan mozzarella
cheese

½ cup (100g) chopped fresh
tomatoes

2–3 servings vegan eggs,
uncooked

½ teaspoon salt

½ teaspoon pepper

Cook the spaghetti according to the package directions.

Preheat the oven to 350°F (180°C).

Cook the crumbles according to the package directions.

In a large oven-safe skillet over medium heat, add the
oil and cook the onions and garlic until softened.

In a large bowl, mix together the cooked onions and
garlic, basil, sauce, ricotta, mozzarella, tomatoes, vegan
eggs, salt, and pepper. Mix in the cooked pasta, and
place the mixture into the same skillet, adding more
oil if needed. Place the skillet into the preheated oven
and bake for 25–30 minutes or until the pie is cooked
through.

CALORIES: 231.6; TOTAL FAT: 10g; SODIUM: 265.6mg; TOTAL
CARBOHYDRATES: 19.8g; DIETARY FIBER: 3.8g; SUGARS: 1.6g;
PROTEIN: 14.5g

Pork Meatballs with Onion Gravy

Fresh rosemary and thyme pair beautifully with the plant-based pork in this dish, even if you only came for the gravy.

Serves 4

24 ounces (680g) Impossible Pork

1 tablespoon (15ml) olive oil

2 large onions

2 cloves garlic, minced

1½ cups (350ml) vegan beef broth

½ teaspoon minced fresh thyme

¼ teaspoon minced fresh rosemary

¼ cup (60g) vegan cream cheese

Form the pork into 16 meatballs, and cook according to the package directions.

In a nonstick skillet on medium-low heat, add the oil and cook the onions, stirring often. Continue to cook until the onions are softened and slightly browned. Add the garlic and cook for another minute. Stir in the remaining ingredients and simmer until the sauce is thickened. Place the cooked meatballs in the sauce to coat. Serve over pasta, noodles, or sautéed cabbage.

CALORIES: 294.6; **TOTAL FAT:** 17.8g; **SODIUM:** 487.8mg; **TOTAL CARBOHYDRATES:** 16.8g; **DIETARY FIBER:** 5.3g; **SUGARS:** 3.8g; **PROTEIN:** 17.5g

Italian Sausage Bake

Once you've grilled your sausage links, pop them in the oven
with the rest of the ingredients, and in less than the time it takes
to get everyone to the table, you'll be ready to eat.

Serves 4

8 links Field Roast Italian Sausage

3 large roasted peppers, sliced

2 cups (400g) diced grape tomatoes

3 tablespoons (45ml) olive oil

2 cloves garlic, minced

1½ cups (42g) fresh spinach

1½ cups (350ml) pasta sauce

½ teaspoon salt

½ teaspoon pepper

Parsley or basil leaves (optional)

Preheat the oven to 375°F (190°C).

On a hot grill, grill the sausages according to the package directions.

Grease an oven-safe baking dish with cooking spray or a little oil. Place the peppers, grape tomatoes, oil, garlic, spinach, sauce, salt, and pepper into the prepared baking dish. Place in the preheated oven and bake for about 15 minutes or until the tomatoes are starting to soften.

Place the grilled sausage into the baking dish and continue to bake for another 10–15 minutes. Garnish with torn basil or parsley leaves and serve over pasta or rice.

CALORIES: 231.9; TOTAL FAT: 12.6g; SODIUM: 479.7mg; TOTAL CARBOHYDRATES: 12.8g; DIETARY FIBER: 3.6g; SUGARS: 4g; PROTEIN: 17.5g

ADDITIONAL RESOURCES

The following articles and online resources will help you make good decisions about eating vegan meat substitutes and find exactly the products you want.

Beyond Meat: https://www.beyondmeat.com/products/

Bobs Red Mill: https://www.bobsredmill.com/

Cooking Light: https://www.cookinglight.com/eating-smart/nutrition-101/what-is-tempeh

The New York Times: https://www.nytimes.com/2020/03/03/dining/impossible-beyond-meat.html

The Economist: https://www.economist.com/international/2019/10/12/
   plant-based-meat-could-create-a-radically-different-food-chain

Entrepreneur: https://www.entrepreneur.com/article/346116

Field Roast: https://fieldroast.com/

Food Service Direct: https://www.foodservicedirect.com/

Gardein: https://www.gardein.com/meatless

Health Line: https://www.healthline.com/nutrition/seitan#avoid

Impossible Foods: https://impossiblefoods.com/

Olive Nation: https://www.olivenation.com/

Thrive Market: www.thrivemarket.com/

Vegan Essentials: https://veganessentials.com/

Very Well Fit: https://www.verywellfit.com/what-is-seitan-4684069

Wikipedia: https://en.wikipedia.org/wiki/List_of_vegetarian_and_vegan_companies

PHOTO CREDITS

CONVERSION CHARTS

METRIC EQUIVALENTS FOR DIFFERENT TYPES OF INGREDIENTS

STANDARD CUP	FINE POWDER	GRAIN	GRANULAR	LIQUID SOLIDS	LIQUID
¾	105 g	113 g	143 g	150 g	180 ml
⅔	93 g	100 g	125 g	133 g	160 ml
½	70 g	75 g	95 g	100 g	120 ml
⅓	47 g	50 g	63 g	67 g	80 ml
¼	35 g	38 g	48 g	50 g	60 ml
⅛	18 g	19 g	24 g	25 g	30 ml

USEFUL EQUIVALENTS FOR LIQUID INGREDIENTS BY VOLUME

¼ tsp	=							1 ml
½ tsp	=							2 ml
1 tsp	=							5 ml
3 tsp	=	1 tbsp	=			½ oz	=	15 ml
		2 tbsp	=	⅛ cup	=	1 oz	=	30 ml
		4 tbsp	=	¼ cup	=	2 oz	=	60 ml
		5⅓ tbsp	=	⅓ cup	=	3 oz	=	80 ml
		8 tbsp	=	½ cup	=	4 oz	=	120 ml
		10⅔ tbsp	=	⅔ cup	=	5 oz	=	160 ml
		12 tbsp	=	¾ cup	=	6 oz	=	180 ml
		16 tbsp	=	1 cup	=	8 oz	=	240 ml
		1 pt	=	2 cups	=	16 oz	=	480 ml
		1 qt	=	4 cups	=	32 oz	=	960 ml
						33 oz	=	1000 ml = 1 L

USEFUL EQUIVALENTS FOR DRY INGREDIENTS BY WEIGHT

(To convert ounces to grams, multiply the number of ounces by 30.)

1 oz	=	1/16 lb	=	28.3 g
4 oz	=	¼ lb	=	113 g
8 oz	=	½ lb	=	227 g
12 oz	=	¾ lb	=	340 g
16 oz	=	1 lb	=	454 g

INDEX